Two Books Are Better Than One!

by Shari Frost

Reading and Writing
(and Talking and Drawing)
Across Texts in
K–2

MAUPIN HOUSE BY
CAPSTONE PROFESSIONAL
a capstone imprint

Two Books Are Better Than One!:
Reading and Writing (and Talking and Drawing) Across Texts in K–2
By Shari Frost

Cover Design: Richard Parker

Developed and Produced by Focus Strategic Communications, Inc.
Adrianna Edwards: project manager
Ron Edwards and Adrianna Edwards: editors
Rob Scanlan: designer and compositor
Francine Geraci: proofreader

Library of Congress Cataloging-in-Publication Data
Cataloging-in-publication information is on file with the Library of Congress.
978-1-4966-0608-2 (pbk.)
978-1-4966-0611-2 (eBook PDF)
978-1-4966-0614-3 (eBook)

Image Credits: Capstone Studio: Karon Dubke, Cover; Design Elements: Focus Strategic Communications Inc.; Shutterstock: Cora Mueller, Peshkova

Capstone Professional publishes professional resources for K–12 educators. Contact us for tailored, in-school training or to schedule an author for a workshop or conference. Visit www.capstonepd.com for free lesson plan downloads.

This book includes websites that were operational at the time this book went to press.

Maupin House Publishing, Inc. by Capstone Professional
1710 Roe Crest Drive
North Mankato, MN 56003
www.capstonepd.com
888-262-6135
info@capstonepd.com

Table of Contents

Chapter Five
Reading and Writing: Connecting Fiction and Informational Texts

Chapter Six
Reading and Writing: Connecting Fiction and Procedural Texts

Chapter Seven
Reading Across Text Types: Connecting Poetry and Informational Text

Acknowledgments

The idea for writing this book emerged from work that I did on a national literacy project. It was pure joy to spend hours on end reading and talking about children's books and creating literacy lessons with a group of literacy gurus. Many thanks to Roberta Buhle, Sunday Cummins, and Deborah Hays for sharing their knowledge and insights with me and for pushing my thinking.

Writing can be a lonely endeavor. One of the most productive weeks in the writing of this book took place during a writers' retreat in the summer of 2015. It was an honor and a privilege to have gifted teacher-writers read and respond to my writing. Their probes, questions, and suggestions challenged my ideas and gently, but persistently, nudged me toward a better version of this book. Thank you Brenda Powers, Stella Villalba, Kate Di Cesare, Gretchen Taylor, Jennifer Schwanke, Carly Ullmer, Jan Burkins, and Kim Yaris.

The classroom stories told in this book came from real classrooms. Many of the lessons or variations of the lessons were taught in those classrooms. I am grateful to the teachers who opened the doors to their classrooms to me and to their literacy coaches who facilitated my gaining entry. Thank you Dianna Balcken, Loretta Edwards, Elenie Grapsas, Emily Hansbrough, Tanesha Harris, Nicole Ivers, Michelle King, Judith Martin, Andrea McCauley, Hillary Morrison, Kiwanna Phillips, Bridget Sawchuk, Candace Schlesser, Zoe Sikorski, Liane Skolak, and Meghan Sweet.

This book would certainly not exist without the patient and loving support of my husband, Art. He listened to me read aloud children's books, tagged along with me on trips to the public library, proofread, encouraged, supported, cajoled, and even stayed up all night to do battle with Microsoft Word's Table of Contents application. You are awesome. I am so lucky.

Introduction

"What happened to Country Frog?" said Celia, with a slight quiver in her voice.

"Maybe he is just hibernating," suggested Adam hopefully, "like Frog did in *Frog and Toad are Friends* [Lobel, 1970]."

"Maybe he changed into something else, like *Farfellina and Marcel* [Keller, 2005]," offered Sophie. "Frogs change, don't they?"

Lori is conducting an interactive read-aloud of the book *City Dog, Country Frog* (Willems, 2010) with her first grade students. She has just read the poignant climax of the book. It is winter. City Dog is frantically running through the fields and around the pond, desperately searching for his friend Country Frog. But the frog is nowhere to be found. City Dog finally settles on a rock and waits, looking very forlorn. Lori asked her students to turn and talk about the climax. What do you think happened to Country Frog? What will City Dog do now? She walks around, listening in on students' discussions.

So what happened to Country Frog? The author, Mo Willems, doesn't actually say. The reader will have to rely on his or her background knowledge or refer to other experiences with books to make an inference. Lori's first graders have spent their school year listening to books, reading books, talking about books, and writing about books. They have learned that if you have a question about something that has happened in a book, it is a good idea to think about what happened in other books. So at this point late in the school year, it is natural for Lori's students to ponder the whereabouts of Country Frog by thinking about other stories that they have read in which someone was looking for a friend.

I applaud the approach taken by Lori's students. I also reflect on my past reading experiences to help me gain a deeper understanding of, and a deeper appreciation for, what I am currently reading. When I read the 2014 National Book Award winning book *Brown Girl Dreaming* (Woodson, 2014), I immediately thought about another book that I had read entitled *The Warmth of Other Suns: The Epic Story of America's Great Migration* (Wilkerson, 2010). In the latter book, the author chronicles what happens to three individuals who migrated from the Jim Crow South to face new challenges in the northern states in the 1930s–1950s. In *Brown Girl Dreaming*, Woodson tells the story of her own family's migration from South Carolina to New York City in the 1960s–1970s.

Lori is helping her students understand that each reading experience functions as a mentor for future reading and writing experiences. After they read *City Dog, Country Frog*, they engaged in several reading, writing, talking, and drawing experiences about the book. Children were surprised to learn that Mo Willems was the author of *City Dog, Country Frog*. They commented that it was very different from his other books. They decided that the biggest difference between *City Dog, Country Frog* and the other Mo Willems' books is that the other books are funny. One child pointed out that Willems was not the illustrator of *City Dog, Country Frog*, and Lori asked them to think about why this was so. They concluded that Willems makes funny pictures and that this book was definitely not funny.

Lori engaged children in a discussion about the relationship between City Dog and Country Frog. Children all agreed that they were very good friends. Lori pushed them, "How do you know that they were good friends?" After the discussion, Lori led her students in a shared writing, charting evidence from *City Dog, Country Frog* that documents how friendships work. They recorded the following entries on their chart:

- Friends play together.
- Friends do favors for each other.
- When your friend goes away, you are sad.
- Friends take turns deciding what they will do together.

Children could not resist making comparisons to Mo Willems' series books about another pair of good friends, Elephant and Piggie (2007–). So Lori invited her students to look for "acts of friendship" in the Elephant and Piggie books.

While engaged in this inquiry, some children looked for "acts of friendship" in the Frog and Toad books as well. Students recorded the "acts of friendship" on sticky notes and posted them on two charts. One chart had copies of the Elephant and Piggie book covers. The other chart had copies of the Frog and Toad book covers. The whole class came together and used the charts to support their discussion about similarities in the friendships across the books.

Finally, Lori asked her students to use what they had learned from their reading and research to write about "What Makes a Good Friend." To support their writing, she encouraged them to use the charts that they had developed together as well as to revisit the Elephant and Piggie books, the Frog and Toad books, *Farfellina and Marcel*, and *City Dog, Country Frog*. Lori reminded the struggling writers that they could use drawing and labeling to augment their writing.

The exploration of friendships did not end with *City Dog, Country Frog*. Whenever children encounter another example of a pair of friends in a book, they inevitably think about how this friendship compares to the friendship shared by City Dog and Country Frog, by Frog and Toad, or by Elephant and Piggie. This ongoing process confirms what they have already learned and adds to their knowledge.

Reading picture books aloud is something that happens in every first grade classroom every day. Reading Frog and Toad books and Elephant and Piggie books is another frequently occurring activity in first grade. Writing about the qualities of a good friend is also rather commonplace. However, reading across texts, having in-depth discussions to identify themes and unifying ideas, and using that information from the multiple texts and text types to support writing take those everyday first grade activities to a whole new level. Even better, these tasks support fledgling readers and writers in developing a reservoir of knowledge about literature and text structures that will nurture their literacy development and take it to higher and deeper levels.

Two Books Are Better Than One!: Reading and Writing (and Talking and Drawing) Across Texts in K–2 will support you in creating the kind of learning experiences for children that you just read about in Lori's classroom. The goal is a school day filled with authentic reading and writing tasks across the curriculum that encourage children to read more, write more, and think deeply.

Each chapter in this book will present a series of anchor lessons connected to the Common Core State Standards (2010) that can be used at the kindergarten through second grade levels. You can use the format of the anchor lessons as a guide for creating your own lessons using the recommended pairs of texts or even paired sets of your own design.

Chapter One

The Why and How of Using Paired Books in K–2

So exactly what are paired books, and what do you need to consider when assembling a paired book set for instruction? A paired book set is composed of two books that go together like milk and cookies, peanut butter and jelly, or cake and ice cream. The books can be related by character, theme, perspective, genre, or perhaps some other characteristic—or simply be written by the same author. When you create a paired book set, have an instructional purpose and an essential question in mind. The essential question drives the reading, writing, and discussion throughout the series of lessons. The instructional purpose shapes the types of tasks that children will be asked to do. Consider how the texts will be read. Will the books be read aloud to students? Or will children read them using shared reading or guided reading? Consider also other literacy lessons and activities that you can teach using the paired book set.

Why should you use paired books? Using paired books helps promote critical thinking, builds children's proficiency in making comparisons and contrasts, and provides additional and varied information on a selected topic. The value of connecting two or more texts, called "intertextuality," has been well documented in educational research. Camp (2000) says that reading paired books allows students to dig deeper into a topic and enhances their comprehension. Soalt (2005, p. 680) says that paired texts are "uniquely suited to scaffolding and extending students' comprehension." Costley and West (2012) state that reading across texts is essential to the success of young readers.

Reading paired books is especially supportive for emergent, early, and transitional readers. The reading of the first book serves as a scaffold for the reading of the second book, making it more accessible to the reader. The reader's confidence is boosted, making it safer for him or her to take risks in constructing meaning from the text. Short, Hartse, and Burke (1996, p. 537) say that reading paired books allows students to "share and extend understandings of each text differently than if only one text had been read and discussed."

Another reason for using paired books in kindergarten through second grade classrooms is that it addresses one of the Common Core State Standards. Anchor Standard 9 for Reading requires students to "Analyze how two or more texts address similar themes or topics in order to build knowledge or to compare the approaches the authors take." This standard cries out for paired books. Gaining proficiency in this standard will eventually support students in career and college readiness skills, such as writing research papers. Many national and state assessments often require students to read two texts, answer questions about the texts, and write an essay using information across the two texts. Students who have been engaged in these types of reading and writing activities since kindergarten will complete these assessments with greater ease.

Finally, using paired books is just sound pedagogy based on extensive research into brain-based learning. Willis (2015) tells us that the human brain is a "pattern-building and detecting mechanism …. Seeking patterns is the brain's way of making sense of information and experiences … We identify new things based on their similarities and relationships to things we already know. The development of literacy takes place in the same way all memories are constructed in the brain—by relating the *new to the known*."

How can we support kindergarten, first grade, and second grade students in reading paired texts and writing using information from those texts? Unsurprisingly, this is best accomplished via the familiar, proven early literacy instructional strategies that you and other primary teachers have used for years.

In future chapters that deal with specific paired book sets, these strategies will be referred to repeatedly but not described, and it will be assumed that the reader is familiar with their implementation. Here, for the sake of completeness, let's review the procedures for each of these strategies and briefly discuss their respective advantages (and disadvantages, if any) in the particular setting of a paired book lesson.

Interactive Read-Aloud

An interactive read-aloud is a reading experience in which you read aloud a book with embedded stopping places for the listeners to *interact* with the text. It encourages and supports children in engaging with their peers and you about the text.

An interactive read-aloud requires planning. It is advisable for you to read through the book several times, sometimes aloud, in preparation for the read-aloud performance. Every time we read to children, we are giving a sales pitch. We want them to buy into the idea that reading is fun. So we give our best performance during read-alouds. You should typically designate two to three stopping places for student interactions. The stopping places are opportunities for children to work toward answering the essential question and respond to what they have heard. Possibilities for stopping places can include opportunities to teach or practice vocabulary, to employ a comprehension strategy, or to identify and discuss literary elements.

An interactive read-aloud uses the classic "before, during, and after" structure of most reading lessons. The "before" phase of the lesson introduces children to the book. The title and the author's name are read, and the cover of the book is displayed. You might want to review some aspects of story grammar. Finally, share the purpose of reading the chosen book and let children know what they will be working on while listening to it.

The interactive read-aloud provides the highest level of teacher support. It is in the "I do, you watch" phase of the gradual release of responsibility continuum (Pearson and Gallagher, 1983). You will do all the reading while children listen and interact during the designated stopping places. With you doing all the "heavy lifting" of the reading, the cognitive load (Sweller, Merriënboer, and Paas, 1998) is lightened for children. They can devote all their energy to comprehending and enjoying the book. The interactive read-aloud is well suited to engaging all students with increasingly complex selections of text.

The "during" phase of the interactive read-aloud features two components—a teacher think-aloud, and actively involving children in interacting with their peers and with you about the book. In a teacher think-aloud, model specific comprehension strategies such as activating

TIP
You might want to flag some or all of the stopping places with sticky notes, each of which could include the specific language that you would like to use while talking to or prompting students at that point in the book.

background, inferring, or visualizing. The strategy modeled is connected to the lesson's objective.

The second component of the during phase includes student interactions, which can take a number of forms. The most prevalent and appropriate form of student interaction for an interactive read-aloud in kindergarten through second grade is "turn and talk." Turn and talk is the go-to strategy in this context because it gives all children an opportunity to share their thinking instead of having most of them passively watch a single interaction between them and you.

To implement turn and talk, group students into pairs. When the reading reaches a designated stopping place, students turn to face each other instead of you and orally respond to the prompt. Students are explicitly taught to engage in the best practices of discussion—take turns, make eye contact, listen so closely that they can retell their partner's thinking, and engage in "conversation moves." The conversation moves include agreeing with, respectfully disagreeing with, and adding onto what their partner has said. Children are taught to begin their responses to their partners via explicit use of a phrase or sentence, such as one of the following:

> "I agree with you because … "
> "I see it another way." (disagreeing)
> "Can you say more about that?" (clarifying)
> "I don't understand what you mean."
> "I'd like to add onto what you've said."

Turn-and-talk lessons and conversation moves are carefully modeled, taught, developed, and practiced over time. Anchor charts are created to support students during the turn and talk. Circulate and listen in on student conversations while they are engaged in turn and talk. After giving students adequate time to discuss the topic, select one or two pairs of students to share what they have discussed. Turn and talk allows every child a chance to say what he or she thinks. It is more equitable than the traditional classroom model of talk, in which you ask a question and one student responds.

The "after" phase of the interactive read-aloud can include a number of activities. First, give children an opportunity to respond to the book orally. Every opportunity should be used to demonstrate that reading is a meaning-making process and that after students have read a text, they carry away a message. A discussion about the text is a great way to accomplish this. It also provides a quick formative assessment of children's comprehension of the text. Then make sure to focus on the essential question. There might be some additional formative assessment to verify that children are making progress toward answering the question.

Another recommended post-reading activity is writing. After children have heard the book, talked about the book, and responded to the book, a great foundation has been laid for a productive writing experience. The writing might even serve as another formative assessment. Types of post-reading writing might include response to the reading, letters to a character or the author, imitating the author's style, or extending the story.

Post-reading experiences can also include extension and enrichment activities. If appropriate, children can retell the text with props. They might also dramatize the text or practice and present a readers' theater. You can engage children in an art activity, drawing, painting, sculpture, or collage.

Of course, reading always leads to more reading. Offering more books on the topic or by the same author for children to read during independent reading time allows for further reading enrichment.

An interactive read-aloud is an excellent choice for paired book lessons at the kindergarten through second grade levels. It allows for more freedom in book selection. Since you are doing the reading and children are listening, the focus of book selection is on the suitability of the book to meet the lesson's objective rather than on the book's reading level. The interactive read-aloud offers an opportunity to expose children to complex texts within their listening comprehension level, which is generally significantly higher than their reading level.

Classic Read-Aloud

You may make the instructional decision to do a classic read-aloud. We are all familiar with a classic read-aloud. It is the kind of read-aloud that parents do at bedtime, that a children's librarian at the public library does at story time, or that you might do as a transitional activity. The purpose of the classic read-aloud is to provide children with the experience of listening to a story (or text) for enjoyment and content. A classic read-aloud is often done prior to an interactive read-aloud. A classic read-aloud might have a brief book introduction and a follow-up discussion. In anchor lessons, classic read-alouds are recommended when reading familiar books, such as traditional tales. A classic read-aloud might also be used when the lessons employ a complex book that will require multiple readings. Questions and discussions are usually limited in a classic read-aloud.

Shared Reading

A shared reading experience is one in which you and children share the task of reading the text. To give children access to the text, the print is usually enlarged. The text might be a big book, a poem written on chart paper, or a digital text projected on a whiteboard. The text is displayed in such a way that all children can see it easily. Offer additional support while the group is reading the text by tracking it with a pointer.

Shared reading is in the "We do" phase of the gradual release of responsibility continuum. Texts that make good candidates for shared reading are those with built-in supportive features, such as rhyme, rhythm, and repetition. These texts invite and encourage children to read along. Even with the supportive features, you may want to read the selected text aloud first before expecting children to read along.

Shared reading is a demonstration of the reading process in action, whereby you demonstrate explicitly how reading works. Track the text, focusing children's eyes on the words that are being read. This reinforces print directionality and concept of word. Tracking also supports children in making a "voice-to-print match" with those all-important high-frequency words. This helps to build students' knowledge of high-frequency words, thereby facilitating automaticity.

Shared reading serves a dual purpose. In addition to presenting the textual content, it also gets students actively involved in learning how to read. To further the latter purpose, any book selected for a shared reading should be read using this technique multiple times—perhaps three to five times—to help children gain proficiency in reading it.

Shared reading has a very high level of student engagement. In the community of a shared reading experience, each child participates at his or her own level of comfort. Children feel safe to take risks. Some children will chime in and read only during the remembered repetitive refrains of the book. Other children will read every single word along with you. The visual feedback (i.e., tracking) and audio feedback make it possible for each child to read just a little more of the text the next time the book is read.

Like the interactive read-aloud, shared reading uses a "before, during, and after" lesson structure. The "before" phase of instruction introduces children to the text. Display the book, reading the title and the names of the author and illustrator. The cover illustration might be discussed. During the first reading, read aloud the entire text without tracking. Children are simply exposed to the text content, the language of the text, and its supportive features. The emphasis of the first reading is on presenting the text content and giving children the support they need to attempt to read the text in a shared environment.

The essential question is addressed in the "during" phase of the lesson. In shared reading, the during phase occurs in the second to perhaps fifth readings of the book. Prior to starting the second reading, children are presented with the essential question. You do a think-aloud, and children are given a purpose for reading. In the second and third (and fourth and fifth) readings, the class works toward answering the essential question, using strategies such as turn and talk.

The lesson will also address some "print-processing" objectives, such as reinforcing high-frequency words, decoding words with a specific phonics feature, or practicing strategies to use when attempting to solve an unknown word. A different print-processing objective can be addressed during each rereading of the text.

✓ TIP

It is a good idea to focus on only one print-processing objective per reading.

The "after" phase of a shared reading activity also has a dual purpose. Information and evidence that help to answer the essential question are documented, and the print-processing lessons are reviewed and reinforced. Post-reading activities to address the essential question would, of course, include a follow-up discussion of the text. And the multiple readings of the text will have prepared children to do some writing in response to it. Like interactive read-alouds, enrichment and extension activities can include any of the following activities:

- visual arts
- literacy centers
- dramatization
- online activities
- video viewing
- much more reading (of course!)

Standard-sized copies of the text can be used in several different ways to reinforce the print-processing lessons. They can be placed in the listening center, giving students additional opportunities to read along. You might even use them for small group instruction. They might also end up in "browsing boxes," a collection of familiar books for children to read as "sponge activities" or during independent reading time. Use sponge activities to engage children in a meaningful task while they are busy with beginning-of-the-school-day tasks, such as attendance, or when some children complete an assigned task before the class is ready to proceed to another task. Finally, children might be allowed to check out the standard-sized copies of the text to take home and show off their reading prowess to their parents.

Shared reading is a great way to increase the level of student involvement in a paired book lesson. A paired book set might consist of two different shared reading texts or a shared reading text and an interactive read-aloud text. A common configuration is a picture book that is used for the interactive read-aloud and a poem that the class reads using shared reading. The essential question is the primary consideration in determining which combination of texts will be used.

Guided Reading

In a guided reading setting, you support and guide a group of four to six children in reading a text. Children are doing the actual reading. It is in the "You do, I'll guide" phase of the gradual release of responsibility continuum. Coach and prompt children as needed in strategy use, word solving, and negotiating the meaning of the text. Also, confirm strategy use and carefully observe children's reading behaviors to gather information for future instruction.

Guided reading groups are generally composed of children with similar instructional needs and/or abilities. However, it is not uncommon to convene a mixed ability group based on interest or strategy instruction. The group is brought together for a specific purpose—the lesson objective. Each child is given his or her own copy of the text and is responsible for reading it in its entirety. There is no round robin reading, with one child reading while the others listen and follow along. Every child reads the whole text. Children who can read silently do so. The other children "whisper read." Confer with as many children as possible while they are reading.

The texts used for guided reading are often "leveled readers." Leveled readers are books especially written for instructional purposes. These books employ a leveling formula based on factors, such as the match between the illustrations and the text, the number of lines of text on a page, and the layout of the text, to determine the difficulty of the book. Match the books to children's reading levels. The criteria used for leveling books can also be applied to trade books, offering an option beyond leveled readers. Since the child is doing the reading, it makes sense to give the child a book that he or she can actually read.

Like shared reading, guided reading will serve a dual purpose. Not only will children be working toward answering the essential question, they will also be working on strategies to support them in becoming strategic and proficient readers. These lessons focus on goals in print processing, increasing sight word vocabularies, developing strategies for solving unknown words, and maintaining comprehension throughout the reading of the text.

The "before, during, and after" structure of the guided reading lesson mirrors some of the procedures for the interactive read-aloud and shared reading—with one big difference. It is the child and not you doing 100 percent of the reading. Your role is strictly supportive.

The emphasis of the "before" phase of the lesson is on preparing the child to read the text. This phase might include several activities. In order to help the child process the print and comprehend the text, you might guide the child in accessing his or her background knowledge on the text's topic and/or model a strategy that the child might find useful. In addition, support the child in examining the structure of the text and the essential text vocabulary. Finally, set a purpose for the reading, probably concluding this element of the lesson with the sentence stem, "Read to find out ... "

The "during" phase of the guided reading lesson consists of children reading and you supporting the readers. While children are reading silently or whisper reading, work your way around the group, listening to each child read and conducting mini one-to-one conferences. In a one-to-one conference between you and a child, the child reads loudly enough for you to hear. Confirm the child's strategy use and support him or her in solving unknown words by prompting the use of an effective strategy. Take notes on your observations of the child's reading behaviors. You will use this piece of formative assessment to help you plan future lessons.

If a child completes the text before you are ready to call the group together for the "post-reading" phase of the lesson, the child might exercise a few options. He or she can reread the text, select another book from the browsing box and read it, or write a response in a reading response journal or in a graphic organizer provided for this purpose.

The "after" phase of the lesson has several components. First, as already stated above, it is always important to communicate that reading is a meaning-making process; after every reading experience, the reader should carry away a message. Hence, it is always a good idea to spend some time talking about what has been read. It gives children a chance to recall the information, organize their thoughts, and articulate them. Listening to what other children have to say about the text's content will help to expand each child's thinking about the text.

Before children begin reading, give them a purpose for reading. Children should be given the opportunity to respond to that purpose. If the purpose of the reading is to "identify the main idea," during post-reading activities, the children should get a chance to tell the main idea.

You should also assess children's progress toward answering the essential question. Chances are excellent that the essential question will be addressed fairly early in the post-reading discussion. If not, be sure to have the class discuss what insights the book offers on the essential question before allowing the post-reading discussion to come to an end.

For children in kindergarten through second grade, word work is a big component of their literacy instruction. The English language is based on the alphabetic principle. It is essential that readers know the letters of the alphabet and the sounds that each letter makes in order to understand their world. Spend a minute or two in the post-reading phase of the guided reading session to work on words. The activity is usually hands-on and interactive. Children might do a word sort, build and break words using magnetic letters, or write words on a whiteboard.

Finally, like the interactive read-aloud and shared reading, you may choose to extend and enrich the guided reading text. These activities may include the following:

- visual arts
- dramatizing
- readers' theater
- center activities
- writing
- more reading (of course!)

The text used for the lesson can be placed in browsing boxes or children's individual book baggies for them to reread during independent reading. Offer children related books to read on the same topic.

Using guided reading in paired book lessons has obvious advantages. Since children are doing the reading, they are more actively involved in achieving the lesson's goals. This is the ultimate goal of reading instruction—to release the responsibility to the reader. Successful experiences in reading across texts in kindergarten through second grade build the confidence necessary for more complex paired book reading and research in later grades.

However, using guided reading for paired book lessons also has a distinct disadvantage. You are limited to books that children are capable of reading. Leveled readers have been criticized for their lack of rich and complex language and ideas or lack of a basic story. As we saw in the Introduction, one of the principles of using paired books is that each reading experience is a mentor for future reading experiences. You want to provide an excellent mentor not only for future reading experiences, but also for future writing experiences.

There are many trade books that have been leveled. In order to minimize or even negate the disadvantage just mentioned above, you might consider using a leveled trade book in a paired reading lesson. But even the trade books that are suitable for the kindergarten through second grade reading levels have their limitations. Therefore, it is a good idea to pair a guided reading book with an interactive read-aloud book. This is essentially what happened in Lori's class. Although it was not mentioned in the Introduction, Lori's students read many of Mo Willems' Elephant and Piggie books in a guided reading setting. And although Lori did not formally engage her class in a paired book lesson, the Elephant and Piggie books (guided reading) were implicitly paired with *City Dog, Country Frog* (interactive read-aloud).

Independent Reading

After shared and guided reading instruction, we give children the opportunity to apply and practice what they have been taught with independent reading. Independent reading texts are those that children can read with no support from you or any other more competent reader. These are texts that children can read with 100 percent accuracy and are generally categorized as "easy texts." Reading easy texts benefits children in numerous ways:

- It boosts confidence.
- It improves fluency.
- It helps to generate positive attitudes about reading.
- It reinforces those important high-frequency words.

You might use several structures for independent reading. Provide children with a book baggie or a book bin. Children, with your support, at least initially, select independent leveled books for the book baggie. Teach them how to find books they can read independently. Standard-sized copies of shared reading books and books used for guided reading often end up in book baggies. "Book shopping" times, when children go to the classroom library to select books for independent reading, are scheduled to refresh the supply of books in the book baggies.

Designate book bins for each of the guided reading groups rather than for each student separately. This is recommended if the classroom library is not extensive enough for each student to carry around several books. Children will recognize their book bin by its color and know, for example, that they are able to read any book in the blue book bin.

You might have "independent reading time." Independent reading time has been given various names, such as "drop everything and read" (DEAR) time, "read and relax," "active reading time" (ART), and "daily independent reading time" (DIRT). Every child in the class sits and reads for a fixed amount of time.

The class sets a reading stamina goal and actively works toward increasing the amount of time that everyone can be actively engaged in reading.

One of the challenges of guided reading instruction is meaningfully engaging children who are not meeting with you. Direct your students to read independently during this time. In this setting, independent reading usually lasts for only one guided reading cycle.

Even though children are reading independently, you play an important role. You need to provide and monitor the books that children are reading. You will probably choose to work on this during reading conferences. The child brings an independent reading book to the conference. Listen to the child read some pages from the book, perhaps take a running record, and have a conversation with the child about the book. From the information gathered at the conference, confirm the child's independent reading level or find evidence that the level needs to be adjusted.

Shared Writing

All paired book lessons include a writing component. In some cases you might choose to use shared writing to address the writing component. In shared writing you and the children collaborate on composing and writing a message. The message is written on a large sheet of paper or projected on a whiteboard. Special care is taken to make sure that every child can see the writing as it emerges.

Shared writing is in the "We do" phase of the gradual release of responsibility continuum. Like shared reading it is an actual demonstration of the writing process. Through shared writing children are able to write a message using the support of the entire class community, especially you, that they would have difficulty writing on their own. Shared writing can be used to write a message in any genre. The length of a shared writing message varies and may take multiple sessions to complete.

A shared writing lesson begins with the selection of a topic. This decision might be made through brainstorming. The topic is often determined by a lesson focus. After the topic is selected, the work of composing the message begins. Group children into pairs or triads so that each child has an opportunity to share his or her thinking through discussion with peers. Then call children together, and make decisions about exactly what the message will say. After the entire text of the message has been orally composed, the work of writing the message begins.

Shared writing, like shared reading, serves multiple purposes. In addition to addressing the essential question, shared writing can also address objectives related to writing, reading, concepts of print, print processing, spelling, and phonics. All of these instructional areas are worked on during the writing of the message.

The act of writing begins by having children point out where the message should begin on the page. Say the sentence. Count out the words in the sentence. Solicit children's input on the spellings and the conventions (capitalization, punctuation, and so on) involved in writing the sentence. When the sentence is completed, the class goes back and rereads the sentence (using shared reading) to ensure that it is satisfactory. The writing of the message continues in this way until the message is complete or the writing reaches an agreed upon stopping place for the session. For instance, a class might use shared writing to construct a class book. The goal for a session might be a page per day.

You do the physical writing of the message. In terminology often used in texts on strategy support, you "hold the pen." If children are involved in writing a word or even a letter, the instructional strategy employed is technically called "interactive writing." The children get to experience the writing process because they have engaged in the following:

- prewriting (conception, brainstorming, topic selection, planning)
- drafting
- revising
- editing
- publishing

Products of shared writing are often displayed on the walls of the classroom or developed into a class book for the classroom library. Children are able to call upon these experiences for support in their own writing.

Anchor Charts

TIP
Samples of anchor charts can be found online.

An anchor chart is a tool to facilitate student self-regulation and to support independence. It is visual evidence of the work done by you and your students—a scaffold that can later be removed as soon as students have learned the lessons reinforced by the anchor chart. An anchor chart plays an important role in K–2 classrooms.

An anchor chart is co-created within the context of a series of lessons. You might teach some lessons on opinion writing, the elements of a story, the procedure for turn and talk, or even a classroom routine. After modeling, practice, and discussion, the chart is made. Along with students, negotiate the language of the chart. Act as the scribe, capturing students' actual words on how to implement the strategy, process, or procedure. The chart is then placed in an area of the classroom where students will use it and have easy access to it. With students, revisit the anchor chart frequently during the first week or two after it is posted. You might have to remind students to refer to the chart. In addition to its instructional value for the specific task at hand, the anchor chart also helps teach an important and more widely applicable lesson about resources that students can use to help themselves.

The teaching practices that are involved in getting an anchor chart launched and used in a classroom include the gradual release of responsibility model. Explicitly state what children will learn and why they need to know it. Then model the desired practice (e.g., turn and talk, how to write a letter, etc.), thinking aloud as you go. Then ask the class to engage in a shared experience of the task. The chart is written over the course of the series of lessons. Have students review the anchor chart before they engage in the desired practice and use the anchor chart afterward to reflect on how well they have succeeded. Monitor students as they attempt the desired practice and provide feedback. Finally, students are ready for independent practice using the anchor chart on their own to self-monitor or remind themselves what to do next.

Anchor charts are posted only as long as children need them. When you are convinced that most children have learned the strategy or procedure, the anchor chart is retired. A smaller copy of the anchor chart can be made available and affixed in notebooks, learning logs, or resource files in specific areas of the classroom.

Reading, Writing, Talking, and Drawing

The lessons in this book will engage children in reading, writing, talking, and drawing. Each represents a component of communication. They are interrelated and interdependent. Each of the reading, writing, talking, and drawing activities will be called to your attention by its own icon.

Reading is the cornerstone of instruction in kindergarten through second grade. It is commonly said that children learn how to read in these grades. The lessons in the book will help you as you engage children in interactive read-aloud, classic read-aloud, shared reading, guided reading, and independent reading.

Writing has a critical role in early literacy. It is one of the ways in which we give information to others. Writing is encoding, which is accomplished in several steps. The sounds that we hear in words are translated into letters, strings of letters are transformed into words, and series of words are used to express thoughts to communicate to others. When children write, they are actively applying all the lessons that you taught them about sounds, letters, and high-frequency words. You should never pass up the opportunity to let them write.

Reading and writing are based on **oral language**. In reading, talk is used to develop and support comprehension. In writing, talk is critical. Students first use talk when they discuss what they are going to write about before they commit it to paper. Then they get to see their spoken words become written words. As Britton (1970) says, "writing floats on a sea of talk."

Drawing is an important bridge to writing. Young children can depict their message through drawing with much more detail and precision than they can by writing. Drawing is also an important form of prewriting for K–2 students. After a child has created a picture, he or she is able to move into writing with greater confidence and ease. Pictures help students know what they want to say.

About the Lessons

Each of the lessons discussed in this book includes two core reading experiences, a writing experience, and additional related lessons. The lessons contain suggested language that might be useful in helping you consider how to approach instructional interactions with students. Additional related lessons are also described, but they are completely optional. Their purpose is to offer opportunities for exploration and engagement on the topic. You should feel free to do as few or as many of them as time and interest allow. The books offered in the lessons are not the only ones that work well for pairing texts. If one of the books suggested in any of the lessons is not available, a suitable replacement can be used.

Chapter Two

Reading and Writing Across Texts About Characters: He's a Real Character

After only a few weeks of kindergarten, children will already have long lists of favorite book characters. The lucky children enter school with their lists, which might include characters, such as Max from *Where the Wild Things Are* (Sendak, 1963), David from *No, David!* (Shannon, 1998), Pete from *Pete the Cat: I Love My White Shoes* (Litwin, 2010), and Nancy from *Fancy Nancy* (O'Connor, 2006). These characters enthrall and delight children. Any read-aloud featuring a favorite character is sure to be a hit.

Characters are literally central to any story. When children learn how to identify characters' traits and motivations, they gain a deeper understanding of the story. Even more important, when they are provided with instruction, support, and practice in character analysis, they become more proficient readers of narratives.

The focus on characters is a great time to do an overall review and reinforcement of the basic story elements (character, setting, problem, and solution). A story elements anchor chart will help children understand these basic story elements, including the critical role that characters have in narratives. If you already have such an anchor chart, it will be useful to refer to it throughout this series of lessons. If you do not already have one, it would be a good idea to co-create one with children after Lesson A-Two below. In the first step for co-creating the chart, ask children to name the people or animals in the story and tell them that these are the characters. Proceed to fill in the "characters" section of the anchor chart. Then ask where and when the story takes place. After receiving students' answers, complete the "setting" section of the anchor chart. Similarly, children are asked to identify the problem in the story, and the "problem" section of the anchor chart is completed. Finally, ask students to tell how the problem is solved. Then fill in the "solution" section of the anchor chart.

TIP

A template for a story elements anchor chart is readily available online.

Paired Book Anchor Lesson Series #1: The Farmer vs. the Duck

Essential Questions

- What clues in a story can help me understand the characters?

- How can thinking about characters help me be the kind of person that I'd like to be?

Featured Books

Click, Clack, Moo: Cows That Type

by Doreen Cronin

Simon & Schuster, 2000

Farmer Brown runs a nice, quiet little farm until the cows find a typewriter that was stored in the barn. Then he starts receiving letters from the cows making all sorts of demands. Should the farmer give in to the animals' demands? *Click Clack Moo: Cows That Type* is the recipient of a 2001 Caldecott Honor award. It was also named to the "Teachers' Top 100 Books for Children" by the National Education Association in 2000 and to the "Top 100 Picture Books of All Time" by the *School Library Journal* in 2012.

Farmer Duck

by Martin Waddell

Candlewick Press, 1992

Running a farm is a lot of hard work. In this story it is not the farmer who does the work. The farmer spends the day lounging in bed, reading, and eating chocolate bonbons. It is the duck that does the work. But the responsibilities of running the farm get to be too much for the duck. The other animals at the farm want to find a way to help their friend the duck. This book received a starred review from *Publishers Weekly* and is a Kate Greenaway Medal recipient. *Farmer Duck* has been called the *Animal Farm* (Orwell, 1946) of the primary grades.

A. Lessons Using *Click, Clack, Moo: Cows That Type*

Lesson A-One: Classic Read-Aloud of *Click, Clack, Moo*

1. Gather children in the whole group meeting area. Position yourself so that every child will be able to see the book. Display the book and read the title and the author's name. This is a good time to review the physical parts of the book (front cover, spine, back cover) if instruction is needed.

2. Accessing Background Knowledge: Some children have limited experiences with farms. You might need to build some background knowledge. If you already have a story elements anchor chart, display it. Then ask any or all of the following questions:

- Look at the cover illustration. Where does this story take place? What is the setting? How do you know?
- What do you find on a farm?
- What happens on a farm?
- Who lives on a farm?
- What is "typing"?

3. Think-Aloud: "Cows that type? I didn't know that cows could type. Hmm, I wonder what the cows are typing. Let's read and find out."

4. Read through the whole story with minimal stopping and discussion, so children can enjoy the story.

Lesson A-Two: Interactive Read-Aloud and Revisiting the Text for Character Study

Rich, high-utility vocabulary words that might be addressed during this reading include *demand, furious, emergency,* and *impatient.* Decide if you want to present the vocabulary before or during the reading. Have a child-friendly definition ready to help children understand each word. Include some of the words on your vocabulary wall, and use them in future morning messages.

1. Tell children that they are going to reread the story. This time they will look closely at the character Farmer Brown.

2. Read the opening page of the story. Call children's attention to Farmer Brown. Have children turn and talk about what they notice about Farmer Brown.

3. Start a character chart about Farmer Brown with his name at the top. Throughout the reading of the story, record the following in separate boxes:

- what he looks like
- what he says
- what he does
- how he feels

4. Read until the end of the page where the first note is posted on the barn (six pages from the title page). Ask children, "What do you think about the note?" Have children turn and talk. Select one or two pairs of children to share their thinking with the class.

5. Read the next page. Ask the following questions:

- What does "went on strike" mean? (when workers refuse to work)
- Where is the text evidence to support your answer? (the letter written by the cows and hens saying that they would not give any milk or eggs unless they got blankets)
- How is Farmer Brown feeling now? (angry)
- How do we know? (text and illustration evidence)
- Does Farmer Brown "have the right" to be angry? Why or why not?

Record the relevant information on the Farmer Brown character chart.

6. Read until the end of the page with the illustration that shows Farmer Brown sitting at a typewriter, 17 pages from the title page. Examine the illustration of Farmer Brown and the content of the note. Identify the word that shows he is angry (*demand*). Record the relevant information on the Farmer Brown character chart.

7. Read the next page. Explore the term "neutral party." Point out the opposing sides: the cows and hens on one side, Farmer Brown on the other side. Make sure children understand that Duck was not on either side. If you can, connect the concept of "neutral party" to real situations that might plausibly arise in children's lives. For example, two of your friends are mad at each other, but you still like both of them. You are a neutral party.

8. Read until the end of the page where the cows and Farmer Brown agree upon a settlement. Have children turn and talk to express an opinion of the settlement. Ask: "Is it fair? Why or why not?" Record relevant information on the Farmer Brown character chart.

9. Read the rest of the book. Ask children to talk about the difference between how the cows and hens got what they wanted and how the ducks got what they wanted. (The ducks got their demands met much more quickly than the cows and hens.) Go back and count the pages chronicling the negotiations between Farmer Brown and the cows and hens. Count the number of notes that were exchanged. Ask the following questions:

   - Why did Farmer Brown give into the ducks' demand so quickly? (He learned from his experience with the cows and hens.)
   - What does this tell us about Farmer Brown? (He is reasonable. He learned from his experience with the cows and the hens.)

   Record the relevant information on the Farmer Brown character chart.

10. Review the Farmer Brown character chart.

11. Start a character trait anchor chart. You will continue to add to this chart as you read other books. Explain that we learn about character traits by looking at what a character says and does. Go back to the Farmer Brown character chart. Point out what has been recorded about what Farmer Brown said and did. Identify two to three character traits to start the character trait chart. Words on the chart might include the following:

   - angry
   - hard-working
   - caring
   - reasonable

REMINDER

If you do not yet have a story elements anchor chart, at this point it might be a good idea to co-create one with your students. Follow the steps described immediately before the start of this lesson series on page 24.

Lesson A-Three: Writing Inspired by *Click, Clack, Moo*—Note Writing

1. Prepare children to write a note to post on Farmer Brown's barn. Go back to the book, and revisit the notes posted on the barn. Point out the basic structure of the notes—greeting, body, closing.

2. Invite student pairs to write a note to Farmer Brown. Give them a chance to talk about what they would like to say to Farmer Brown. Have a few children share their ideas. Make an effort to check in with struggling writers to make sure that they have ideas for writing.

3. Distribute letter writing paper. To provide additional assistance to emergent writers, you might provide a template that includes a space for a picture, the greeting (Dear Farmer Brown), blank lines for the message, the closing (Sincerely), and a blank line for the child's name. See a letter writing template on page 29.

4. Cut out a barn shape from red bulletin board paper. Post "the barn" on a classroom wall. Invite children to post their notes to Farmer Brown on the barn.

5. After children have learned about the format of letter writing, you might suggest letter writing as an option at the writing center or during independent writing, writing workshop, or journal writing.

Optional Literacy Lessons and Activities Related to *Click, Clack, Moo*

1. Word Study

Use picture or word sorts with -*ick* and -*ack* words (for example, *chick, stick, kick, sick, brick, lick, back, black, quack, snack, pack,* and *tack*). You can also start a *cl-* blend word chart. Label it "Click Clack Words." When children encounter words with *cl-* in their reading, record them on the chart. Plan to include *cl-* words in your morning message as well. Some possible words for your "Click Clack Words" chart are *clap, club, closet, close, class, claw, clay, clean, clear, clever, climb, clip, clock,* and *clothes.*

2. Readers' Theater

Create a simple script from the story. Characters can include a narrator, Farmer Brown, the cows, the hens, and the duck. You can include all children in your class by making them cows, hens, or ducks. Have the stronger readers read the parts of Farmer Brown and the narrator. Practice until polished, and then perform it for other classes.

3. Story Elements

Create a story elements graphic organizer for *Click, Clack, Moo.* Have children complete the graphic organizer.

TIP

Display the story elements anchor chart for extra support.

4. Close Reading

Pose the text-dependent question: "Why did Farmer Brown finally decide to give in to the animals' demands?" Children might say the following:

- He wanted milk and eggs.
- He was tired of fighting with the animals.
- He did not want more of the animals to start making demands.
- He cared about his animals and did not want them to be unhappy.

Reread and collect text evidence to support children's answers.

5. Story Sequence Pocket Chart

Make sentence strips of the major events in the story. Include an image on each of the sentence strips to support children in reading them. Have students arrange the sentence strips in order.

Dear Farmer Brown,

_____

_____

_____

_____

_____

_____

Sincerely,

_____

6. Retelling Center

Create a *Click, Clack, Moo* retelling center. You can use a borrowed toy farm or collect props such as toy cows, hens, ducks, and a farmer from a dollar store. Use a red box to make the barn. Invite children to retell the story using the props.

7. Video Viewing

There are several video presentations of *Click, Clack, Moo* available on the Internet, including a **PBS** version. Preview the available versions, and choose one that you like to show to your students.

8. More Reading

Click, Clack, Moo was such a beloved book that Doreen Cronin (the author) and Betsey Lewin (the illustrator) ended up creating a whole series of books based on these characters, especially Duck. Children who are capable of reading at text level M can read these books independently or in guided groups. Some of the books include *Giggle, Giggle, Quack; Duck for President; and Dooby, Dooby, Moo.*

B. Lessons Using *Farmer Duck*

Farmer Duck presents another farmer character, almost a direct contrast to Farmer Brown. The lesson plan presented here is a shared reading lesson plan. However, if your students can read books at text level K, you can use guided reading groups instead.

Lesson B-One: Classic Read-Aloud of *Farmer Duck*

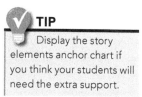
TIP

Display the story elements anchor chart if you think your students will need the extra support.

1. Gather children in the whole group meeting area. Hold up a copy of *Click, Clack, Moo*. Ask children to recall the character Farmer Brown, using these questions during the discussion: "What was Farmer Brown like? What were his character traits?" (He was hard working, caring, and responsible.) "What was Farmer Brown's problem?" (The animals went on strike and would not give him any milk and eggs until he gave them electric blankets.) Tell children that they will read a story about another farmer.

2. Display the big book *Farmer Duck* on an easel. If you do not have a copy of the big book version, you can use a document camera to project a standard-sized or digital book onto a screen.

3. Introduce the book. Read the title and the author's name. Briefly discuss the cover illustration. If none of the children mention it, point out that it is unusual for the farmer to be a duck and not a person. Tell children, "We will read the book and find out why a duck is doing the farm work."

4. The purpose of the first reading is to "get the story into children's heads." Children will learn the repetitive refrain, which will support them in reading along in subsequent readings. Read the entire story with energy and enthusiasm. Allow only minimal discussion and questions. Do not track the text on this first reading. At this point in the lesson, you want children to concentrate on the content of the story rather than the print. Children are likely to chime in at the lines, "How goes the work?" and "Quack!"

Lesson B-Two: Shared Reading of *Farmer Duck* and Character Study

REMINDER

Oral cloze is an oral reading strategy in which you pause before reading a word that you think students might be able to supply. If children know the missing word, they "chime in."

1. Gather children in the large group meeting area for the second reading of the book. This time encourage them to read along with you, especially during the repetitive refrain. Tell them to pay close attention to the farmer because when the reading is done, they will discuss him.

2. Lead children in reading the book. Track the text with a pointer to help children make the voice-to-print match. Use oral cloze to prompt children to join in on the reading. This is a standard shared reading practice.

3. The story has some rich vocabulary that is worth addressing. You might want to take time to pause and discuss some or all of the following words: *fetched, weepy, wriggled,* and *fled*. Give children a chance to talk about what the words mean. Provide them with child-friendly definitions. Include some of the words on your vocabulary wall, and use them in future morning messages.

4. Engage children in a post-reading discussion. Have them turn and talk about the farmer. Open the book to one of the pages where the farmer is prominently featured. Ask children the following questions:

   - What do you think of the farmer? (He is lazy and greedy.)
   - What kind of person is he? (He is a mean person because he makes the duck do all of the work.)
   - What did you see or hear that made you think that? (He never gets out of bed. He never does any work.)

   Call children back together to share their thinking. Make a list of descriptors that children generate. This list will be helpful in the next lesson, particularly when updating the character trait chart.

Lesson B-Three: Creating the Character Chart

1. Lead children in another shared reading of *Farmer Duck*. Tell them, "This time we will make a list of the things that the farmer is doing." By this third reading, almost all children will be able to read most of the book.

2. Start with an empty list. Stop on each page in which the farmer appears. Carefully examine the illustrations. Have children turn and talk about what they see. Call them together, and add the relevant information from that page to the list. By the end of the book, the list will include the following:

   - lying in bed
   - reading the newspaper
   - eating chocolate bonbons
   - sleeping

3. After the book is completed, prepare a character chart for Farmer Duck, starting with an almost identical template to the one you used for Farmer Brown; the only difference will be the name at the top. Solicit children's input while filling in the chart. Write descriptors for the following:

   - how the farmer looks (He's not neat. He needs a shave.)
   - what the farmer says (One sentence: "How goes the work?")

- what the farmer does (lies in bed, naps, eats chocolates, reads the newspaper)
- how the farmer feels (tired, sleepy, has no energy, hungry, lazy)

4. Display the character traits chart that was created in Lesson A-Two. Add more words to the chart, such as *lazy, greedy,* and *mean.* Many of the added words will come from the list that was compiled at the end of the previous lesson. From the two books combined, there will now likely be about seven or eight words on the chart. Return the character traits chart to its place on the classroom wall. When you read other stories, identify the character traits of the characters in those books and add them to the chart.

Optional Literacy Lessons and Activities Related to *Farmer Duck*

1. More Shared Reading

Conduct one to two more shared readings of *Farmer Duck.* Connect one skill or strategy lesson to each rereading of the story. Lessons that can be taught using this book include the following:

- prediction
- cause and effect
- sequence

Skills that can be taught using the book include the following:

- high-frequency words
- onomatopoeia

2. More Reading About Farmers and Farms

Farmer Duck is not the only book that Martin Waddell has written about a farmer. Waddell is also the author of *Pig in the Pond* (1996). This book features a farmer with a very different personality from the farmers in the other books. This will allow you to add more character traits to the chart. The book is available in big book format, making it suitable for shared reading. *Pig in the Pond* is a text level G, so it is also suitable for guided reading.

The books listed below are recommended informational books about farmers and farms. They are appropriate for guided reading and independent reading:

Book Title	Author	Text Level
Cows	Sheri Doyle	H
Diary of a Farmer	Angela Royston	L
Farm Animals	Nancy Dickmann	E
Farmers Help	Dee Ready	L

3. Shared Reading with Cloze Procedure

Cover some strategic words with sticky notes in *Farmer Duck.* Have children use context clues to solve each missing word. Offer a clue if necessary by revealing the first letter of the word.

4. High-Frequency Words

Have children identify the high-frequency words that appear in *Farmer Duck*. Practice words, such as *the, and, with, to, was, did, from, put, up,* and *said,* or practice the words from the book that also appear on your word wall.

5. Listening Center

Put standard-sized copies of *Farmer Duck* in your listening center along with an audio recording of the book.

6. "Duck at Work" Pocket Chart Activity

Make sentence strips naming the work tasks that Duck performed on the farm and, separately, create images depicting each of these tasks. You might include the following:

- Fetch the cow.
- Bring the sheep from the hill.
- Put the hens in the house.
- Wash the dishes.
- Pick the apples.
- Cut the wood.

Have children match the phrases with their corresponding images. Another pocket chart activity can engage children in matching the name of each farm animal to an image of the animal.

7. Retelling Center

Use almost the same toys, figures, and props that you used for the *Click, Clack, Moo* retelling center on page 30. You'll also need sheep and pigs. Invite children to retell the story of *Farmer Duck* using props.

8. Independent Reading

Most kindergarten children will be able to read *Farmer Duck* after multiple shared readings. Put standard-sized copies of *Farmer Duck* in their independent book baggies and browsing boxes. Encourage children to check the book out to take home and read to their parents.

9. Video Viewing

Share a video presentation of *Farmer Duck* with your students. There are several available online. A quick search should yield several good choices.

C. Connecting *Farmer Duck and Click, Clack, Moo* Through the Lens of Character

Post-Reading Discussion

Gather children in the whole group meeting area. Display both character charts—the one listing Farmer Brown's character traits and the one listing the character traits of the farmer in *Farmer Duck*. Give children an opportunity to turn and talk about both farmers and the way that they treated the ducks in the stories. Call them together for a whole group discussion. Invite them to share their opinions of the two farmers. Encourage them to use the language on the character charts.

Comparing and Contrasting the Farmers

Steer the conversation toward looking at the similarities and differences between the two farmers. Engage children in completing a Venn diagram comparing and contrasting the two farmers. If your students can do this activity without support, you might make it a small group or individual task. If your students need your guidance, create a large Venn diagram on a whiteboard or chart, and complete it as a shared experience. First, ask students to tell you how the farmers are alike. Record what they tell you in the overlapping circles space. Then, record how Farmer Brown is different from the farmer in *Farmer Duck* in the circle parts that do not overlap.

Learning About Ourselves from the Stories

 Engage children in one final discussion about the farmers. Make the character charts and the Venn diagram viewable. Say, "Story characters help us think about the kind of person we want to be and the kind of person we do not want to be." Do a shared writing documenting what children learned from the farmers about the kind of people they want to be. This final writing activity can be also done as guided or independent writing.

Other Paired Book Sets Featuring Memorable Characters

The paired book sets listed below also feature characters with contrasting personalities and are recommended for comparing characters across texts. They can be used for additional lessons later in the year or even as alternatives to the lessons presented in detail above.

The Extrovert and the Quiet Yet Powerful Introvert

1. *Katie Woo: Boss of the World* by Fran Manushkin
   Katie Woo is a spunky first grader. She means well but somehow always ends up getting into trouble. This book is an early chapter book. If you choose to read it aloud, you will want to read a chapter at a time. The text level for this book is J, so you might be able use it in guided reading too. It is a series book, so children who enjoy this book will be delighted to learn that there are many more.

2. *Stand Tall, Molly Lou Melon* by Patty Lovell
   Molly is a little funny looking. She is short, has fuzzy hair, buck teeth, and a terrible singing voice. However, Molly quietly stands her ground with bullies and is also able to forgive them. This is a great choice for interactive read-aloud, discussion, and writing.

The Brave and the Fearful

1. *Scaredy Squirrel* by Melanie Watt

   Scaredy Squirrel never leaves his tree. It's far too dangerous out there in the world. He is armed with his emergency kit to help him survive any possible encounter with tarantulas, aliens, or killer bees. This book is a text level L, so many second graders will be able to read it in guided reading groups. It is also an excellent read-aloud.

2. *Sheila Rae, the Brave* by Kevin Henkes

   Louise is in awe of her big sister, Sheila Rae. Sheila Rae isn't afraid of anything—not the big black dog down the street nor thunder and lightning. Sheila Rae fearlessly walks backward to school—with her eyes closed! This book is a good interactive read-aloud.

The Cheerful and the Grumpy

1. *Pete the Cat: I Love My White Shoes* by Eric Litwin

   Pete takes a walk wearing his favorite white shoes. Even though he steps in things and gets his shoes dirty, he remains cheerful. It's a wonderful choice for shared reading.

2. *Prickly Jenny* by Sibylle Delacroix

   There is just no pleasing Jenny. She demands to be left alone, yet she cries when her mother goes away. She is unhappy about what her mother picks out for her to wear and even about the ice cream served for dessert. This book is a good choice for interactive read-aloud.

The Generous and the Selfish

1. *The Spiffiest Giant in Town* by Julia Donaldson

   George the giant buys himself a wonderful new outfit—shirt, pants, shoes, and a tie. Now he is "the spiffiest giant in town." On his way home, dressed in his new clothes, he encounters animals that need his help. This is a good choice for reading aloud and follow-up discussion.

2. *The Selfish Giant* retold by Roberto Piumini

   The Giant returns home after a seven-year absence. While he was gone, children played in his garden. He immediately builds a high wall to keep children out. The consequences of his actions are unexpected and far-reaching. This is a wonderful interactive read-aloud. This book is available through public libraries, Amazon, and eBay.

The Determined and the Defeated

1. *Flight School* by Lita Judge

   Penguin proclaims that he has "the soul of an eagle" and is determined to learn how to fly. He acquires a pair of red goggles and enrolls in flight school. The results of his efforts are disappointing, but he has good friends to help him out. This book is a great read-aloud.

2. *A Perfectly Messed-up Story* by Patrick McDonnell

Louie tries to tell a story, but it keeps getting messed up. The mess gets so big that Louie finally gives up. This is a good book for interactive read-aloud.

Chapter Three

Reading and Writing Across Texts About Central Message (Theme): The Value of Work

When you think of "themes in literature," what comes to mind? Do you flash back to your high school English class? There was that essay question on the final exam for that stuffy, classic canon that the class had spent six weeks reading. The question was, "What is the theme of the story?" You thought you needed to write a lot because that question was worth 20 points. You sat there stymied and confused. These kinds of experiences foster the common belief that theme is a complex concept that is best addressed in high school or maybe even later.

However, kindergarten is not too early to lay the foundation for students to identify the theme of a story. Almost any narrative text has a message about life for the reader to carry away. We read about the experiences of the characters and decide, "I'll never do that," or resolve, "Wow, I should try to do that." If we take the time to talk about a story with 5 year olds, they can tell you its message. Just imagine what second graders can do!

The Common Core State Standards pave the way to learning about themes by asking our young readers to identify the "central message" of a story. That sounds a little less intimidating than theme, doesn't it? For the first lessons in central message, select books with obvious messages, such as fables and other traditional literature. Learning about central message early supports critical thinking and helps prepare students for work on similar topics later on in their school careers.

Paired Book Anchor Lesson Series #2: The Value of Work

Essential Questions

- Why is work important?

- Why is it important to help with work?

Featured Books

The Little Red Hen: A Retelling

by Christianne C. Jones
Capstone, 2011

This retelling of *The Little Red Hen* is a simple yet true to the original classic folktale. It is especially written to be accessible to early readers. The little red hen decides to make bread. She asks for assistance from her housemates—a dog, a cat, and a mouse—in making the bread. They refuse her at each step in the bread-making process. Finally, the bread is done. Who should get to eat the bread?

The Little Red Hen Makes a Pizza

by Philemon Sturges
Dutton Children's Books, 1999

In this popular variant, the little red hen is in the kitchen again. This time she is making a pizza. She needs to do a lot of shopping, chopping, mixing, stirring, and kneading. Her neighbors—a duck, a cat, and a dog—refuse to help her with any of these chores. When the pizza is done, will she share it with her neighbors? This book is the recipient of a 2000 Golden Kite Award.

A. Lessons Using *The Little Red Hen*

This book is written at text level I. If your students cannot read at this level, do an interactive read-aloud or a shared reading of the digital version of the book instead. If your students are able to read books at a higher text level, you might do a guided reading lesson of *The Little Red Hen* by Lucinda McQueen (text level K) instead. If you make any of these substitutions, the steps explicitly listed below will not apply with respect to the details, but they can still be used as a model for constructing lessons.

Lesson A-One: Guided Reading of *The Little Red Hen*

Post a story elements anchor chart, if you have one, near the table where you meet with small groups.

1. Gather a group of up to six children at the table. Do a quick strategy lesson that will be useful to children. An appropriate word solving strategy for level I readers is chunking words into syllables. Give children a word card with the word *gardening* written on it. Have them draw lines to divide it into syllables (e.g., *gar/den/ing*). Remind children that this is a strategy that they can use when they encounter an unknown word.

2. Display the cover of the book for children. They will be able to read the title. Ask them to read it together. Read the name of the author.

TIP

Your anecdotal notes, observations, and running records are the best resources for determining strategy instruction for your groups.

3. Give each child a copy of the book. Tell children to read it through page five and stop. Putting a small sticky note on page five of each copy will help to remind children to stop. Ask them to name the characters and the setting of the story. Refer to the anchor chart.

   Tell children that there is a repeated refrain in this story. Some children might even know the refrain. Have them go to page 13 and read these sentences together:

   > *"Not I," said the cat.*
   > *"Not I," said the dog.*
   > *"Not I," said the mouse.*

4. Set the purpose for reading. Refer to the anchor chart again. Remind children that they know the characters and the setting of the story. Now they are going to read to find out the "problem." Instruct them to read through page 15 to find out what the problem is. Children who can read silently should do so. Those who are still learning to read silently should read in a soft or whispering voice.

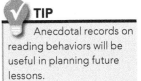

TIP
Anecdotal records on reading behaviors will be useful in planning future lessons.

5. Listen in on each child's reading, one student at a time. Confirm the child's use of strategy. (e.g., "You went back and reread when you found the sentence confusing.") Coach and support the child when he or she encounters difficulty. (e.g., "What can you try? Do you see any chunks that you know?") Record anecdotal notes on children's reading behaviors.

6. Call children back together. Have them turn and talk about the story's problem. Select one child to share the story's problem. Tell them that they should continue reading until they have finished the book and have found out how the problem was resolved. Continue to listen in and conference with individual children.

7. When all children have completed the book, call them back together. Revisit the strategy lesson, asking if anyone used the strategy. Share examples of student use of the strategy that you observed. Remind children that they have named the character, setting, and problem in the story. Refer to the anchor chart again, and ask them to turn and talk about the story resolution. Select a child to share the story resolution.

8. Children will be eager to share their opinions of the little red hen's decision not to share the bread. Give them an opportunity to talk about it. Tell them that they will be doing more talking and some writing about the little red hen's decision.

Lesson A-Two: Revisiting the Book to Determine the Central Message

1. Pair up children. Have them retell the story of the little red hen to each other using "five-finger retelling," as follows:

   - Point to the thumb, and name the characters.
   - Point to the pointer finger, and name the setting.

- Point to the tall finger, and tell what happens at the beginning of the story.
- Point to the ring finger, and tell what happens in the middle of the story.
- Point to the pinkie, and tell what happens at the end of the story.

2. Walk around the room, listening in on the pairs and supporting children who need help.

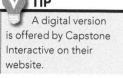

TIP

A digital version is offered by Capstone Interactive on their website.

 3. Call children back together. Since they have read and retold the story, they are familiar with the story details. Project the book onto a screen, using a digital version or a standard-sized book and a document camera. Tell children that the class will look to see what the dog, cat, and mouse are doing while the red hen works. Look at pages 6, 12, 13, 17, 21, and 25. Record the animals' actions on chart paper or the whiteboard. On page 25, the illustration shows the dog, cat, and mouse strongly refusing to help.

 4. Display pages 30 and 31 on the screen. Select a child to read these pages aloud to the class. Ask children, "How do you think the dog, cat, and mouse are feeling? What are they thinking right now?" Have them turn and talk. Select two or three pairs of children to share their discussions with the class.

 5. Ask children, "What do you think the dog, cat, and mouse learned?" Again, have children turn and talk. Select two or three pairs of children to share their discussions with the class.

 6. Ask children the following questions:
- What message do you think the author has for us? (The dog, cat, and mouse did not get any bread because they would not help.)
- What does the author want us to learn from this story? (Everyone should help with the work.)
- What did you learn from this story? (I should help with the work.)

Have children turn and talk and share out one more time.

 7. Collaborate on the oral composition of the central message starting with, "The central message of *The Little Red Hen* is ...." Engage children in a shared writing of the central message. You should be able to capture the central message in only a single sentence.

Optional Literacy Lessons and Activities Related to *The Little Red Hen*

1. Vocabulary

The Little Red Hen uses some rich vocabulary for the word *said*. The words used include the following:
- exclaimed (page 18)
- shouted (page 25)
- muttered (page 26)
- yelled (page 29)

Have children read the sentences in the book that contain *exclaimed*, *shouted*, *muttered*, and *yelled*. Encourage them to mutter when they read the sentence with *muttered* and to exclaim when they read the sentence with *exclaimed*. Post the words on the vocabulary wall. Use these words in interactions with children. (e.g., "Dana exclaimed, 'It's recess time.'" She exclaimed because she was excited.") Challenge children to find other words that mean *said* in their small group and independent reading.

2. Readers' Theater

The Little Red Hen is the perfect book for readers' theater in kindergarten through second grade. There are parts with limited and repeated language that will allow struggling and emergent readers to participate. The repeated reading and performance all contribute to fluency building. The read-along helps to solidify high-frequency word vocabularies. When doing readers' theater, put children in groups of five—the narrator, the little red hen, the dog, the cat, and the mouse. Write your own script or find one online. Give children a few days to practice. Have a "premiere week," and schedule one performance per day.

3. Word Study

Reading *The Little Red Hen* is the perfect time to review and reinforce the /e/ sound. Many children struggle with the /e/ sound. For these children the anchor words *red* and *hen* will provide useful support. For example, build words in the *-en* and *-ed* word families, do picture and word sorts with *-en* and *-ed* words, or create a "red hen" word family chart with the *-ed* and *-en* words for children to refer to when reading and writing.

There are also several examples of words with inflectional endings in the book (e.g., *lived, asked, helped, cleaning, cooking, gardening*). Early readers are sometimes challenged by these endings. Give them practice adding inflectional *-ed* and/or *-ing* onto high-frequency words that they know.

4. Story Sequencing

Create images of the steps that the little red hen went through to make the bread. Affix them to cardstock to make them sturdier. Have children put the bread-making steps in order. This activity can be done with a pocket chart.

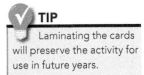

TIP
Laminating the cards will preserve the activity for use in future years.

5. Dramatize the Story

Provide the actors with "hats" made of sentence strips. Write the name of the appropriate character on each sentence strip. Affix either an image of the character or animal ears (dog ears, cat ears, mouse ears). Have children dramatize the story in groups of four.

6. Read Other Retellings

Once children have read one version of *The Little Red Hen*, other versions will be easy for them. Collect a variety of little red hen stories. Stick to the original version for now. Variants will be explored later in this series of lessons. Have children vote for their favorite version.

7. Planting Wheat

Get some wheat berries from a local health food store. Soak the berries in water for 10–12 hours. Give each child a paper cup. Fill each cups three-quarters full with potting soil. Plant the soaked berries, one for each cup. Wheat berries are fast growing. Have children keep a wheat plant journal. Each day have children draw a picture and write a sentence documenting what is happening with their plant.

8. Shared Reading of *Bread, Bread, Bread*

Bread, Bread, Bread (Morris, 1989) is available in big book format. Read about the different ways that people eat bread around the world.

9. How Do You Help?

None of the animals in the story were willing to help the little red hen. Our classrooms are filled with children who love to help, and they will enjoy an opportunity to talk and write about how they do so at home and at school. Here are several ways you can help them do so:

- Give children a chance to talk about how they help at home and at school.

- Provide each child with a sheet of paper that has a box for an illustration at the top of the page and lines for writing at the bottom. If necessary, you can provide the sentence frame, "I help _____."

- When children complete their writing, let them share in small groups of three or four. That way everyone will get a chance to share. This writing can also be included in a class book called "We Help."

B. Lessons Using *The Little Red Hen Makes a Pizza*

Lesson B-One: Classic Read-Aloud of *The Little Red Hen Makes a Pizza*

1. Gather children in the large group meeting area. Display the cover of *The Little Red Hen Makes a Pizza*, which is likely to generate an enthusiastic response. Many children will be able to read the title. Encourage them to try. Read the name of the author. Ask children to recall what happened in the other little red hen story. (The hen did all the work, and the other animals would not help.) Ask them to show a thumbs-up if they think that the other animals in this book will help and a thumbs-down if they think that the other animals will not help.

2. Read the story all the way through without stopping for instruction.

Lesson B-Two: Interactive Read-Aloud of *The Little Red Hen Makes a Pizza*

For this read-aloud lesson, you will be keeping track of all the different kinds of work that are involved in making bread. Have a "Help Wanted" chart prepared to assist in accomplishing this. You can simply write "Help Wanted" on the whiteboard. If you write it on a piece of chart paper, you can use it for other lessons in this series as well.

1. Read aloud the first page of the story. Have children identify the words that connect this story to the original little red hen story. ("The Little Red Hen had eaten the last slice of her tasty loaf of bread.")

2. Stop again after reading the third page after the title page (the duck, cat, and dog jumping rope). Ask students if they thought that the other animals were actually refusing to help the little red hen. (No, they were saying that they didn't have a pizza pan.)

3. Continue reading aloud through the seventh page after the title page (the duck, cat, and dog getting ice cream from the ice cream truck). Talk about the nature of the red hen's request. What kind of help does she want? What does she want the other animals to do? Start charting on chart paper or the whiteboard the kind of help that she is requesting. Record the answer on the chart.

4. Continue reading aloud through the eleventh page after the title page (the animals having a barbecue). Go back to the "Help Wanted" chart. Ask children what kind of help the little red hen wants and what she is asking the animals to do. Record the answer on the chart.

5. Continue reading aloud through the fifteenth page after the title page (the animals playing in the water from the fire hydrant). Return to the "Help Wanted" chart. Again ask children what the little red hen is asking the animals to do to help her. Record the task on the chart.

6. Continue reading aloud through the twenty-third page after the title page (all the animals eating the pizza). Here the author poses the question, "Now can you guess what the duck, the dog, and the cat each said?" Have children turn and talk to share their guess with a partner. Then take the pulse of the class. What do children guess the animals said?

7. Finish reading the book aloud. Look at the chart to determine where the little red hen needed assistance. The list will include borrowing a pizza pan, going to different stores, and tasks related to making the pizza. Have children turn and talk about why the little red hen shared her pizza with the other animals.

Lesson B-Three: Revisiting the Book to Determine the Central Message

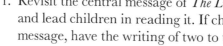

1. Revisit the central message of *The Little Red Hen*. Display the shared writing, and lead children in reading it. If children independently wrote the central message, have the writing of two to three preselected children available. Ask those children to read their writing to the class.

REMINDER
Remind children that the central message is a lesson that we learn about life from a story

2. Have children turn and talk. Ask them if they think the central message of *The Little Red Hen Makes a Pizza* will be the same or different. Remind them that they will need to give reasons for their answer. Circulate, listening in on the conversations.

3. Call children back together. Have one to two pairs of children share their thinking. Children will report that *The Little Red Hen Makes a Pizza* will have a different message because the story has a different outcome.

4. Ask children what we learn from *The Little Red Hen Makes a Pizza*. Have them turn and talk. Circulate and listen in on the pairs. Prompt and encourage, as needed. Identify children who have good ideas to share.

5. Call children together to share their ideas. Then make an effort to have every child write the central message of the story. The shared writing experience of the central message of *The Little Red Hen* will serve as a scaffold for children. Allow for their different levels of developmental writing. Encourage reluctant writers to draw and label a picture before they start to write the central message. In some cases their ideas will not be completely clear from their writing, and verbal communication will be needed to clarify their thoughts about the central message. Try to get each child to write at least one sentence. Circulate while children are writing. After observing their writing, select two to three children who will be asked later to share their ideas about the central message with the class. Select messages that are reasonable based on the story yet somewhat different from each other.

6. Call children together. Ask the two to three children who were selected in the previous step to read their central messages to the class.

Optional Literacy Lessons and Activities Related to *The Little Red Hen Makes a Pizza*

1. Store Sort

   The little red hen had to go to three different stores to get the supplies that she needed for making the pizza. Get children to talk about what kinds of things are sold in each store. Create a sort for items that you buy at the following stores:
   - the hardware store
   - the delicatessen
   - the grocery store

   This sort can be done in a pocket chart in groups or as a cut-and-paste task for individuals.

2. The Little Red Hen Cooks Again

There is yet another little red hen story called *Cook-a-Doodle-Doo!* by Janet Stevens and Susan Stevens Crummel (2005). In this book the little red hen makes a strawberry shortcake. This book is a text level N. Second graders reading at this level or higher can read this book independently or in guided reading groups. Read it aloud to kindergarten and first grade classes.

3. *Little Red Henry*

Sometimes a character does not want or need help. Read aloud this story of a boy who was getting far too much help. *Little Red Henry* by Linda Urban (2015) opens the door to conversations about independence.

4. Sequencing

Recreate the images from the book and write captions using the words in the text.

5. Procedural Writing

Revisit the pages in *The Little Red Hen Makes a Pizza* that describe how she made the pizza. Talk about how the directions help you know what to do. Put children in groups of two or three, and have each child tell his or her group about something that he or she knows how to do (e.g., make a snowman, feed the dog or other pet, set the table, water plants, or play a game). Provide a procedural writing template for children who require extra support with either spaces for writing or boxes for drawing. Circulate and support children while they are writing.

6. Write Your Own Variant

Philemon Sturges and Janet Stevens took the little red hen story and wrote their own versions. They changed the food that the red hen makes and the kinds of animals that refused to help. Your students can write their own red hen story. This activity can be done individually or together in a shared writing experience. In the prewriting planning process, pick the characters, pick the food that the hen will make, and list the steps needed to make the food. Engage in a brief conversation about the theme of the revised story, which should remain the same as the theme of the original book. Then let the writing begin.

7. Pizza My Way

The little red hen put pepperoni, olives, mushrooms, onion, garlic, and anchovies on her pizza. Ask children to write about what they like on their pizza.

C. Connecting *The Little Red Hen and The Little Red Hen Makes a Pizza*

Story Comparison Chart

 Use the Little Red Hen Story Comparison Chart as a model (see the template on page 47), or enlarge it to complete with children. Talk about the similarities and the differences between the two stories. Record the information on the chart. Display the chart in the classroom along with the two books read for this series of lessons and other versions of the little red hen.

What Would You Do?

 In *The Little Red Hen*, the hen refused to share the bread that she made because the other animals did not help her. In *The Little Red Hen Makes a Pizza*, the hen shared the pizza with the other animals even though they did not help her. However, they agreed to wash the dishes when they were done eating. Ask children, "What would you do? If you asked your friends for help and they refused, would you be willing to share what you made?" Put children in pairs, and let them explain their positions.

Opinion Writing

 After the conversations, it is time for children to commit their opinions to writing. Draw children's attention to an opinion writing anchor chart (if you have one). Review the components of opinion writing. Pose the question, "Should the little red hen share her food?" If your students require extra scaffolding, provide them with the opinion writing template (see page 48 for a sample). Support them in stating their opinions, giving reasons for their opinions, and writing a concluding sentence. Allow for a range of developmental levels of writing. Encourage children to draw and label to support their writing.

> **TIP**
> You may want to co-create an opinion writing anchor chart with your students after the completion of this activity.

Little Red Hen Story Comparison Chart

Title (Book Cover)	Characters	Setting	What kind of help did the Little Red Hen want?	What did the Little Red Hen make?	Did the Little Red Hen share?	What is the central message?

Name _____

My Opinion

I think:

_____

_____

_____

_____

_____

_____

Reason:

_____

_____

_____

_____

_____

_____

Closing sentence:

_____

_____

_____

_____

_____

_____

Other Paired Book Sets for Comparing Central Messages

Here are some other pairs of books with central messages that invite comparisons across texts. Like the little red hen stories, some of the pairs offer children an opportunity to look at two sides of an issue and talk, draw, and write about their opinions.

The Value of Work

This pair of books has the same two central messages as the featured pair. One character works, and the other character does no work but wants to benefit from the work.

1. *The Ant and the Grasshopper* by Mark White

   This retelling of the Aesop fable with the same title is a text level I book. That makes it accessible to most second graders and some first graders for guided or independent reading. The ant works hard all summer long gathering food, while the grasshopper plays. Then winter comes. How will the grasshopper survive?

2. *Frederick* by Leo Lionni

   Frederick the mouse lives in a community of mice. The other mice work hard all summer gathering food for the winter. However, Frederick sits around collecting nontangible things like colors, thoughts, and feelings. When the winter comes, the other mice confront Frederick. What will he contribute to the community for the winter? This book is suitable for an interactive read-aloud.

Honesty Is the Best Policy

1. *The Boy Who Cried Wolf: A Retelling of Aesop's Fable* by Eric Blair

   This retelling of the famous Aesop fable is written at text level I. A shepherd boy entertains himself by getting the townspeople to come running whenever he calls for help to protect his sheep from a wolf. The text level makes this a good choice for guided reading in most second grade and some first grade classrooms.

2. *The Empty Pot* by Demi

   The emperor of China has no children to continue his dynasty. So he distributes seeds to all children of China, but with a challenge. The child who grows the best plant will be the heir to the throne. This book is suitable for interactive read-aloud.

Kindness

1. *Each Kindness* by Jacqueline Woodson

   Maya is the new girl at school. Instead of making her feel welcome, Chloe and her friends call her names and refuse her invitations to play at recess.

Chloe's teacher teaches the class an important lesson about being kind. Does Chloe learn the lesson in time? This book is suitable for interactive reading.

2. *Stick and Stone* by Beth Ferry

Stick rescues Stone from a bully, and they become fast friends. Then Stick finds himself in a trouble. Will Stone be able to help? Simple, rhythmic, rhyming text makes this a good choice for shared reading.

Perseverance

1. *The Carrot Seed* by Ruth Krauss

A boy plants a carrot seed and continues to take care of it even after everyone tells him that it "won't come up." This book is a text level G, making it an excellent choice for shared, guided, and independent reading in grades K–2.

2. *The Girl and the Bicycle* by Marc Pett

A girl sees a bicycle in the store window and falls in love. She counts her saved money, scrounges for loose change, and does extra chores to earn money to buy the bicycle. This book is a wordless picture book, which increases the opportunity for talking. The story would also make an excellent shared writing project with children supplying the text.

Cooperation

1. *Swimmy* by Leo Lionni

This is a classic story of how the little fish Swimmy gets all the other little fish to work together to accomplish a big task. It is a good book for an interactive read-aloud.

2. *The Enormous Turnip* by Bridie McBeath

The farmer grows a turnip, which is so big that it takes everyone working together to pull it up. This version is a text level E, making it a good choice for guided reading in kindergarten and first grade. There are numerous versions of this folktale available at various text levels. There are also several variants, including the following:

- *The Enormous Watermelon* by Brenda Parkes and Judith Smith (1986). This story features characters from Mother Goose rhymes and is excellent for shared reading.
- *Big Pumpkin* by Erica Silverman (1992). This seasonal book is available in digital format, making it an excellent choice for shared reading. It is a text level J, so it is also a good choice for guided reading at the first and second grade levels.
- *Jamie O'Rourke and the Big Potato* by Tomie dePaola (1992). This seasonal book is a text level L. Your reading options include guided reading for second grade and interactive read-aloud.

Chapter Four

Reading and Writing Across Texts with Different Perspectives: Whom Do You Believe?

The old adage says, "There are two sides to every story." Few of us ever considered the wisdom of this adage when it came to traditional stories until Jon Scieszka gave us the wolf's perspective in The True Story of the 3 Little Pigs by A. Wolf (1989). Whether you believed the wolf's side of the story or not, it opened the door to discussing perspective in the early elementary grades. Children who learn to consider perspective as early as kindergarten are on a firm foundation for becoming critical consumers of news, advertising, and research.

These lessons will serve as a foundation for future lessons on perspective. Children will be introduced to the idea of point of view and will learn to differentiate between these two cases:

- the character tells his or her own story (first person)
- an "invisible storyteller" tells the story (third person omniscient)

Children will learn to look for clues that help to determine who is telling the story. They will realize that after the identity of the storyteller is established, it is important to examine his or her character traits. Can we believe what this character is telling us? Is he or she reliable? Why or why not? Stories told by an invisible storyteller (third person omniscient) are generally assumed to be reliable. Well, at least we used to think so …

Paired Book Anchor Lesson Series #3: Whom Do You Believe? (Point of View)

Essential Question

- Who is telling the story, and can we believe him or her?

Featured Books

Little Red Riding Hood
by Jerry Pinkney
Little, Brown Books for Young Readers, 2007
Caldecott-winning illustrator Jerry Pinkney retells this gentle, beautifully illustrated version of the traditional tale. This retelling contains all of the basic elements of the original Grimms' telling without the blood and gore.

Honestly, Red Riding Hood Was Rotten!: The Story of Little Red Riding Hood as Told by the Wolf (The Other Side of the Story)
by Trisha Speed Shaskan
Capstone, 2012
The wolf tells his side of the Red Riding Hood story. This wolf claims to be a vegetarian who would normally never go near meat in any form, animal or human. However, there were extenuating circumstances. He hadn't eaten in weeks, and Red Riding Hood reminded him of his favorite food in that red hooded cloak—apples!

The format of this series of lessons will be slightly different from that of the previous lessons. Both stories will be read aloud to children rather than using shared or guided reading for one of the books. To help focus children's attention on the contrasting stories' perspectives, no activities will be done between reading the two stories.

A. Lesson One: Classic Read-Aloud of *Little Red Riding Hood*

1. Gather children in the whole group meeting area. Position yourself so that every child will be able to see the book. Display the book and read the title, *Little Red Riding Hood*, and the author's name, Jerry Pinkney.

2. To activate background knowledge, call children's attention to the cover illustration. Ask any or all of the following questions:

   - What does the illustration tell us about the character? (If no one mentions it, talk about the red hooded cloak.)
   - What does the illustration tell us about the setting? (winter, the woods, the "olden days")
   - Do you know the story of Red Riding Hood? If you do, raise your hand. Now think about what you remember about the story. We will see if this story is like the version that you know.

3. Read the entire story with minimal stopping and discussion so that children can get the story content and enjoy it.

B. Lesson Two: Interactive Read-Aloud of *Honestly, Red Riding Hood Was Rotten!: The Story of Little Red Riding Hood as Told by the Wolf (The Other Side of the Story)*

1. Read this book the following day or later on the same day so that children will easily be able to recall the story events of *Little Red Riding Hood* (Pinkney, 2007). Gather children in the whole group meeting area. Position yourself so that every child will be able to see the book. You have the option of projecting the book onto a screen or reading from a standard-sized book. Display the book and read the title, *Honestly, Red Riding Hood Was Rotten!: The Story of Little Red Riding Hood as Told by the Wolf (The Other Side of the Story)*, and the author's name, Trisha Speed Shaskan.

TIP

The book *Honestly, Red Riding Hood Was Rotten!: The Story of Little Red Riding Hood as Told by the Wolf (The Other Side of the Story)* is also available in digital format.

2. Point out that this version of the Red Riding Hood story is very different from the one that was read earlier. Have children turn and talk about the differences that they are noticing already. After children are done sharing, call them back together and jot down some of their ideas.

3. As a think-aloud, say, "The title is giving us a hint about who is telling the story. I'm thinking that the storyteller is not very nice. What word in the title makes me think that the storyteller is not very nice?" (He is calling Red Riding Hood names: rotten.) "Listen carefully to the story, and see if you can figure out who the storyteller is."

4. Read the entire story, minimizing stops for questions and discussion so that children can get the story content and enjoy the story.

C. Lesson Three: Identifying the Respective Storytellers and Connecting the Texts by Comparing the Storytellers' Levels of Reliability

1. When the second story is complete, have children turn and talk about who is telling the story in this book and how they know. Select a child to identify the book's storyteller. Then select other children to find additional evidence that the wolf is the storyteller as you go through the book.

2. Now display *Little Red Riding Hood* (Pinkney, 2007). Tell children that "an invisible storyteller" is telling this story. Explain that an "invisible storyteller" (third person omniscient perspective) is used to tell many stories. Say, "We can tell when the story is told by an invisible storyteller because the words in the text include 'he,' 'she,' 'they,' and 'them' instead of 'I' and 'me.'" Show some samples of familiar class favorites that are written in the third person omniscient perspective. Possible examples can include the following:

   - *The Gingerbread Man*
   - *Goldilocks and the Three Bears*
   - *The Three Billy Goats Gruff*

3. Display both Red Riding Hood books and say, "We are going to think about the storytellers in each book. Can we believe what the storytellers are telling us? Can we trust the storytellers? Why or why not?"

4. Display your character trait anchor chart that you co-created with your students in Chapter Two (see page 27). If necessary, review the listed character traits. Hold up *Little Red Riding Hood* (Pinkney, 2007). Ask a volunteer to state who is telling the story (invisible storyteller). Refer to the character trait anchor chart. Ask children whether we can identify any character traits of the invisible storyteller. (No. He or she is invisible. We do not know anything about the invisible storyteller. Therefore, we cannot add any of his or her traits to the character trait anchor chart.) Then ask children to turn and talk about whether they trust the invisible storyteller and whether they believe what he or she told us about what happened to Red Riding Hood. Invite volunteers to tell what they talked about.

5. Now display or hold up a copy of *Honestly, Red Riding Hood Was Rotten!: The Story of Little Red Riding Hood as Told by the Wolf (The Other Side of the Story)* (Shaskan, 2011). Tell children that they will go through this book and identify character traits of the storyteller, the wolf. Stop at each of the following pages so that children can turn and talk to decide which character trait the wolf is exhibiting and then record the information:

    *   the cover (mean)
    *   page 10 (dishonest, lying)
    *   page 11 (dishonest, lying)
    *   page 14 (dangerous, vicious, greedy)

6. The reading of *Honestly, Red Riding Hood Was Rotten!: The Story of Little Red Riding Hood as Told by the Wolf (The Other Side of the Story)* is not complete without addressing what happened to Red Riding Hood and her grandmother. Say, "What does the Big, Bad Wolf want us to believe about Red Riding Hood and her grandmother? Why?" (He wants us to believe that Red Riding Hood and her grandmother are not nice people. Then we won't feel so bad when he eats them.)

7. Ask children whether they believe the Big, Bad Wolf. Distribute paper to children. Ask them to write about whether they believe the wolf's side of the story. Remind them that they must tell the reasons why or why not. Children who would benefit from an additional scaffold can take a position: "I believe the Big, Bad Wolf because ..." or "I do not believe the Big, Bad Wolf because ...." (See sentence frames on pages 55–56.)

Name _____

```


```

I believe the Big, Bad Wolf because

_____

_____

Name ______________________________

I do not believe the Big, Bad Wolf because

____

____

Optional Literacy Lessons and Activities Related to the Red Riding Hood Stories

In previous chapters, optional additional activities were provided for each of the two books separately. Here, however, the suggested optional activities are applicable to both books collectively rather than being specific to either one of them.

What Would You Bring to Grandmother?

Reread the first pages of the stories. Ask children what Little Red Riding Hood brought her grandmother (chicken soup and raisin muffins; cake and butter). Ask, "What would you bring to your grandmother if she were not feeling well?" Children can draw their response, draw and label their response, draw and write their response, or write their response.

Favorite Clothes

Go back to the books. Read aloud the sentences describing how Red Riding Hood feels about her red hooded cloak. Point out to children that Red Riding Hood loved her red hooded cloak and wore it everywhere. Ask them, "What is your favorite clothing item?" Let them turn and talk about it. Model writing a short piece about *your* favorite clothing item. (It would be great if you were wearing it.) Have children draw and write about their favorite clothing item. Provide paper with space for drawing at the top. The following questions might help:

- Who gave it to you?
- What store did it come from?
- Were you there when it was purchased?
- Did you pick it out?
- Why do you like it so much?

Story Retelling

Engage children in retelling the Red Riding Hood story. You can do the following:

- Use the five-finger retelling method with pairs of children:
- Point to the thumb and name the characters.
- Point to the pointer finger and name the setting.
- Point to the tall finger and tell what happens at the beginning of the story.
- Point to the ring finger and tell what happens in the middle of the story.
- Point to the pinkie and tell what happens at the end of the story.
- Use stick puppets. Have children color them, cut them out, and attach each of them to a craft stick. Use the figures to retell the story.

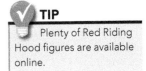

TIP
Plenty of Red Riding Hood figures are available online.

Readers' Theater

Create your own script using the language from the book, or find a suitable script online. Children can practice during independent work time and perform for the class when they are ready.

Red Riding Hood Stories

Listening to two readings of another Red Riding Hood story is an excellent scaffold for children to read the story independently or in a guided reading group. Here are some versions at various text levels:

Book Title	Author	Text Level
Little Red Riding Hood	Maragret Hillert	E
Little Red Riding Hood	Harriet Ziefert	G
Little Red Riding Hood	Karen Lee Schmidt	M

"The Other Side of the Story" Series

Capstone has a series of traditional tales told from the perspective of another character, often the antagonist. All of these books are available in digital format. Some of them are written at text level P, making them good choices for interactive read-alouds in most K–2 classrooms. Some of them are included in the final section of this anchor lesson. Here are some others that your students might enjoy:

- *Frankly, I Never Wanted to Kiss Anybody!: The Story of the Frog Prince as Told by the Frog (The Other Side of the Story)* by Nancy Loewen
- *No Kidding, Mermaids Are a Joke!: The Story of the Little Mermaid as Told by the Prince (The Other Side of the Story)* by Nancy Loewen
- *No Lie, I Acted Like a Beast!: The Story of Beauty and the Beast as Told by the Beast (The Other Side of the Story)* by Nancy Loewen
- *Really, Rapunzel Needed a Haircut!: The Story of Rapunzel as Told by Dame Gothel (The Other Side of the Story)* by Jessica Gunderson

Homonym Hunt

Honestly, Red Riding Hood Was Rotten!: The Story of Little Red Riding Hood as Told by the Wolf (The Other Side of the Story) begins with the Big, Bad Wolf saying, "My tail is different. Did I say tail? I meant tale." This opens the door to talk about homonyms. Go through the next page of the text. Start making a paired list of the words in the text that have homonyms followed by their respective homonyms (e.g., *red/read, bare/bear, too/two* and *to, one/won, right/write, meat/meet, not/knot, nose/knows*). Invite children to continue the list with words from the core lesson texts and their independent reading books.

Informational Books About Apples

Below are several informational books about apples:

- *An Apple's Life* by Nancy Dickmann, Heinemann, 2010
- *Apples* by Erika L. Shores, Capstone Press, 2016
- *Apples Grow on a Tree* by Mari Schuh, Capstone Press, 2011

Red Riding Hood Across Cultures

Here is a list of Red Riding Hood stories representing different cultures that are suitable for classic or interactive read-alouds:

- *Flossie and the Fox* (This is a Southern African American Red Riding Hood.) by Patricia McKissack, Dial Books for Young Readers, 1986
- *Lon Po Po: A Red-Riding Hood Story from China* by Ed Young, Philomel, 1989
- *Petite Rouge: A Cajun Red Riding Hood* by Mark Artell, Dial Books for Young Readers, 2001
- *Pretty Salma: A Little Red Riding Hood Story from Africa* by Niki Daly, Clarion, 2007

Other Paired Book Sets for Presenting Same Story/Different Viewpoints

Below are some pairs of books with contrasting viewpoints. As in *Honestly, Red Riding Hood Was Rotten!: The Story of Little Red Riding Hood as Told by the Wolf (The Other Side of the Story)* and *Little Red Riding Hood*, they offer children an opportunity to consider two sides of a story and assess the reliability of the storytellers.

Both Sides of the *Three Bears* Story

1. *The Three Bears* by Paul Galdone
   The Bear family takes a walk while waiting for the porridge to cool. While they are gone, Goldilocks enters their home and wreaks havoc.

2. *Believe Me, Goldilocks Rocks!: The Story of the Three Bears as Told by Baby Bear (The Other Side of the Story)* by Nancy Loewen
   We have always believed that Goldilocks was a bit of a brat. However, Baby Bear—whose name is Sam—comes to her defense. Goldilocks is really a good girl who enters the Bears' house on a dare. By the way, Sam does not like porridge.

Both Sides of the *Jack and the Beanstalk* Story

1. *Jack and the Beanstalk* by Steven Kellogg

   Jack and his mother are destitute. She sends him to the market to sell their last possession, a cow. Jack uses the proceeds of the sale to buy some magic beans. His mother is furious and throws the beans out of the window. In the morning there is a huge beanstalk that reaches up to the sky.

2. *Trust Me, Jack's Beanstalk Stinks!: The Story of Jack and the Beanstalk as Told by the Giant (The Other Side of the Story)* by Eric Braun

   The giant has not had an easy life. He has been called "fatso" and "stinky." Then he has to deal with Jack's breaking into his house and stealing all his treasures. It's just not fair!

Both Sides of the *Cinderella* Story

1. *Cinderella* by Marcia Brown

   This is the classic telling of the Cinderella story complete with glass slipper, evil stepmother, and fairy godmother.

2. *Seriously, Cinderella is SO Annoying! The Story of Cinderella as Told by the Wicked Stepmother (The Other Side of the Story)* by Trisha Speed Shaskan

   Could we have been all wrong about Cinderella? Her stepmother says that she chatters incessantly, lies habitually, and tries to foist her chores off on others. The only reason that she was not allowed to go to the ball was that she was hoarse from all of that talking.

Both Sides of the *Princess and the Pea* Story

1. *The Princess and the Pea* by John Cech

   The prince is ready to get married. Although he meets many beautiful and gracious maidens claiming to be princesses, none of them have the elusive quality that would make them a "real princess." Then one stormy night, a maiden comes to the door ...

2. *The Very Smart Pea and the Princess-to-Be* by Mini Grey

   Did you really think that anyone could feel a pea through 20 mattresses? If you were skeptical, this book will provide some insight. The pea tells the real story.

Books About Family Members with Different Perspectives

The following are not paired book sets. In each case the contrasting viewpoints are contained internally within a single book.

1. *The Pain and the Great One* by Judy Blume

   The Pain (little brother) is messy, noisy, and gets away with murder. His big sister is sure that their parents love him more. The Great One (big sister) is bossy, a showoff, and always gets her way. Her little brother is sure that their parents love her more.

2. *What Mess?* by Tom Litchenfeld

   A mother confronts her son about his messy room. However, the boy does not think the room is messy at all.

Chapter Five

Reading and Writing: Connecting Fiction and Informational Texts

It is generally agreed that authors write fiction to entertain and inspire readers. In the midst of reading and enjoying a story, questions often emerge for the reader. When reading *Caps for Sale: A Tale of a Peddler, Some Monkeys, and Their Monkey Business* (Slobodkina, 1985), children might wonder if monkeys really do mimic the actions of others, and, if so, why? Does the expression "monkey see, monkey do" describe reality? When listening to the story *Officer Buckle and Gloria* (Rathman, 1995), children might become curious about police canine units. What a wonderful learning opportunity!

We know that the best learning comes from natural curiosity. When the impetus for inquiry is authentic, the level of engagement increases tremendously. In such cases, children are more likely to retain the information that they learn. There are techniques that you can use to spark that natural curiosity. This opens the door to teaching children about informational books, text features, and the inherent differences between reading for information and reading for entertainment.

A well-chosen fiction picture book can set the whole process in motion. This lesson series begins with just such a book. It is guaranteed to raise questions.

Paired Book Anchor Lesson Series #4: Tell Me More!—Exploring Concepts from Books

Essential Questions

- How can I use informational books to help find answers to my questions about stories?
- What is hibernation?

Featured Books

Bear Snores On

by Karma Wilson
Margaret K. McElderry Books, 2002
Bear Snores On is an international best-selling book about a bear hibernating in a cave. While he sleeps his friends drop in for a visit. A spontaneous party breaks out, but Bear continues to sleep throughout the festivities. This charming story is told in rhyme, further endearing it to young listeners.

Why Do Bears Sleep All Winter? A Book About Hibernation

by May Englar
Capstone, 2007
This is a classically constructed informational book on hibernation. It is complete with a table of contents, glossary, index, and all the text features that support inquiry. A special feature is the scientific inquiry template included in the book. Children can use this structure to conduct future inquiries. Please note that if you are unable to find this book, there are several other options you can use to adapt this lesson:

Hibernation
by Tori Kosara
Scholastic, 2012

Hibernation
by Robin Nelson
Lerner, 2011

Hibernation
by Margaret Hall
Capstone, 2006

A. Lessons Using *Bear Snores On*

Lesson A-One: Classic Read-Aloud of *Bear Snores On*

1. Gather children in the whole group meeting area. Position yourself so that every child will be able to see the book. Display the book and read the title, *Bear Snores On*, and the author's name, Karma Wilson.

2. To help activate children's background knowledge, call children's attention to the cover illustration. Have children turn and talk about what is happening in the picture. Circulate to listen in on several of the conversations. Identify a pair of children who mention hibernation. In the whole group share, ask that pair to introduce the concept of hibernation. You might say, "Hibernation? That's an interesting idea. Let's read and find out if this bear is hibernating. Maybe we'll also find out more about hibernation."

3. Read the story aloud all the way through so that children will get the story content. You might briefly pause at the repetitive refrain "But Bear snores on" to encourage children to join in.

4. After the book has been completed, have children turn and talk again, this time about what they learned about hibernation from the book. Give the pairs a chance to share out with the whole class. You can limit the length

of the share session by asking, "Does anyone have something different to share? Something we have not heard yet?" You might also pause after each comment and ask, "Did anyone else learn the same thing? Raise your hand if you did."

5. Take notes on students' comments for a hibernation inquiry chart. This chart can be used in future lessons.

Lesson A-Two: Interactive Read-Aloud of *Bear Snores On* to Explore Text Types

1. Call children together for a second reading of *Bear Snores On*. This time you can confirm or briefly point out the hibernation facts, but the major focus of this reading will be on the text type. Ask children if the book is fiction or informational (nonfiction) if you have already introduced this concept. If you have not, this is a great time to introduce it. Display a fiction anchor chart that shows the features of fiction texts. Tell children that as you read the story, there will be a stopping place every few pages to collect evidence that *Bear Snores On* is a fiction book.

2. Read through the fourth page after the title page. (The illustration shows Bear asleep in an underground lair covered with snow surrounded by bare aspen trees.) This time children are sure to join in on the repetitive refrain. Have children turn and talk about indications that this is a fiction book. At this point the only hint that the book is fiction is the pot and kettle in the bear's lair.

3. Read through the next repetitive refrain. Again ask children to turn and talk about indications that this is a fiction book. They will say that the mouse talks and builds a fire.

4. Read through the next repetitive refrain. Continue the pattern of asking children to turn and talk about indications that this is a fiction book. They will say that the hare is talking and that the hare and mouse are popping corn and brewing tea.

5. Read through the next repetitive refrain. Again ask children to turn and talk about indications that this is a fiction book. This time tell them that the class has already noted the talking animals. Encourage them to look for other evidence. They will say that the badger is carrying a bag of treats.

6. Do not stop at the next repetitive refrain because the next segment does not offer any new indicators. Read aloud through the twenty-fifth page after the title page. (The illustration on the *previous* page shows Bear awake and growling at the animals while they run away from him.) Ask children to turn and talk about how Bear is feeling and how they know this from the illustrations and the author's words. You might want to take a minute to look at all the words for "cry" *(whimper, wail, blubber)*. Point out that the talking, crying bear is another piece of evidence that the book is fiction.

7. Finish the book. Confirm that the book is fiction. If you started a new fiction anchor chart at the start of this lesson, record some indicators of fiction books. Even if you displayed an existing anchor chart at the start of the lesson (see #1 above), you will probably be able to add some new indicators to it.

B. Lessons Before Reading the Second Book

The transition time between the two books, including the time spent on the next two lessons, should be short. The intervening time should always be less than a week, and the shorter the better. So do your best to minimize it.

Lesson B-One: Preparing for Inquiry

1. Using the notes that you took on children's comments at the end of Lesson A-One, prepare a chart of the "hibernation facts" that they mentioned. Display the chart so children can see it, and lead them in a shared reading of these hibernation facts. Provide a child-friendly definition of hibernation. For example, "Hibernation is the way that some animals survive the cold weather and lack of food in the winter. They find a place underground or in a cave and stay there until winter ends. They sleep, hardly breathing, and their body temperatures get very low. They stay that way until warmer weather comes."

2. Ask children to turn and talk about questions that they have about hibernation.

3. Distribute half sheets of paper. Have children record their questions about hibernation on the paper. Encourage them to use drawing, labeling, and developmental writing—whatever they need to commit their questions to writing. Collect the questions. Read each question aloud to the class, skipping over duplicates that will arise when multiple students ask essentially the same question. Some students' possible questions are listed in the next lesson.

Lesson B-Two: Categorizing Hibernation Questions

1. Prepare and provide the class with a list of the questions generated by students at the end of the previous lesson. The list can be recorded on chart paper, a standard page can be projected on a screen, or you can use any other medium that accomplishes the same purpose. Here are some sample questions that children might have asked:

   a. Why do animals hibernate?
   b. Which animals hibernate?
   c. How long do they hibernate?
   d. Where do they hibernate?
   e. What will happen if they don't hibernate?
   f. Is it hard to get bear cubs to go to sleep in the winter?
   g. Do they wake up to use the bathroom?
   h. Will a loud noise wake them up?
   i. Do hibernating animals get cold?
   j. Do hibernating animals get hungry?
   k. How do hibernating animals get protection from their enemies?

2. Have children look at the list of questions and suggest categories for grouping them, provided that they are able to do so. This will be beyond the capabilities of some K–2 children. If that is the case with your students, preselect the categories yourself, or at least suggest one or two categories on your own to start students off. Since the categories will depend on the list of questions, it would be impossible to specify them in advance. However, a reasonable set of categories for the above list of sample questions might include the following:

TIP
Note that there will almost always be an "Other" category to catch a small number of one-of-a-kind questions.

- Who, where, and why? (sample questions a., b., and d.)
- What do hibernating animals need? (sample questions i., j., and k.)
- Waking (sample questions c., g., and h.)
- Other (sample questions e. and f.)

 3. Go through the questions one at a time. Talk about each question, and have students tell you which category it belongs to and why.

 4. Prepare another chart with children's questions grouped into categories. You might choose to use a pocket chart. Lead children in a shared reading of the questions about hibernation. Ask them how they will find the answers to their questions. Someone will say "Read a book." Hold up *Bear Snores On*. Ask children if they can find the answers to their question in this book. When they reply "No," remind them that *Bear Snores On* is a fiction book, and fiction books are written to entertain. Tell them that they will need another kind of book to find the answers to the hibernation questions. They will need an informational book.

C. Shared and Interactive Reading and Shared Writing of *Why Do Bears Sleep All Winter? A Book About Hibernation*

TIP
This task will work best if you obtain an LCD projector and project the book onto the screen. You will want children to see the text features.

The read-aloud of this informational book will be very different from a read-aloud of a fiction book. It will not be read word for word from cover to cover. This read-aloud will actively demonstrate how an informational book is read when the reader is seeking the answers to specific questions. Carefully map out your plan for this lesson. Decide how many read-aloud sessions you will need to devote to the task. You will need to determine how many questions you will answer during each session.

1. Hold up the book *Why Do Bears Sleep in the Winter? A Book About Hibernation*. Read the title. Ask children if they think that this is a good book to find the answers to their questions. They will undoubtedly agree that it is. Read the author's name. Then project the book onto the screen.

2. Project the page containing the table of contents onto the screen. Find out if anyone can name the page and explain its function. If no one can, provide the information. (This page is called the table of contents. The table of contents lists all the topics in the book and gives the page number for each topic.)

3. Project the page with the index onto the screen. Find out if anyone can name the page and explain its function. If no one can, provide the information. (The index is found at the end of the book. It is a list of

important words and phrases in the book, and it provides page numbers where you can read about each word or phrase.)

4. Project page five onto the screen. Read it aloud. Ask children why this process sounds familiar. Hopefully, someone will say that this is what they are currently doing. Explain that observation is one way to investigate, but they are investigating by reading to find the answers to their questions.

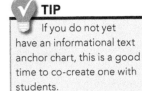

5. Ask children if the book is fiction or informational (nonfiction). Display an informational text anchor chart if you have one. Ask children how they know the book is an informational book. Refer to the informational text features throughout the inquiry.

6. Read the first hibernation question. For example, select the question "Why do some animals hibernate?" Project the table of contents onto the screen. Tell children that the table of contents will show them the right page to turn to in order to find the answer to this question. Have them read along with you as you read the table of contents. Pause after each entry. Tell children to give a thumbs-up if they think that the answer to the question will be in this section. If not, they should give a thumbs-down.

7. After you have identified the correct section—"Why Do Some Animals Sleep All Winter?"— on page 7 of the book, turn to that section and read it aloud to children. Point out the informational text features present on those pages:

- headings
- sidebars
- photographs
- bold print
- glossary words encountered

8. After children have heard the pages read aloud, ask them to turn and talk about the answer to the question. Circulate and listen in on some of the conversations. Select one pair to share out with the whole class. Ask children to give a thumbs-up or a thumbs-down to indicate whether they agree or disagree with the answer.

9. Lead children in a shared writing of the answer to the question on your chart. When the answer is written down, lead children in a shared reading of it.

10. Continue in this manner, repeating steps 6–9 above until you have answered all the questions. This may take four to six sessions, depending on your students' stamina. There might be some questions that are not answered in the book. Talk about options for finding the answers to those questions, such as in other books, websites, and so on.

11. If you started a new informational text anchor chart in step 5 above, record some indicators of informational texts. Even if you displayed an existing anchor chart at step 5, you will probably be able to add some new indicators to it.

12. A list of books that you might use to answer other questions about hibernation can be found on page 23. Here are some others that might help:

- *All About Animals in the Winter* by Martha E.H. Rustad, 2016
- *Animal Hibernation* by Jeanie Mebane, 2013
- *Hibernation* by Robin Nelson, 2011
- *What Is Hibernation?* by John Crossingham and Bobbie Kalman, 2002

D. Informative/Explanatory Writing About Hibernation

Your students have now read books and engaged in inquiry about hibernation. The inquiry emerged from reading a fiction book. The reading, questioning, and writing that they have done will serve as prewriting for this task. They can use the information from their inquiry to do their own informative/explanatory writing.

1. Distribute writing paper on which the top half of the page has a space for drawing and the bottom half of the page has lines for writing. Tell children to explain hibernation based on what they know. They can refer to the chart and to the books that they used. They can make a picture at the top of the page. Ask them to be sure to label their picture.

2. Circulate while children are writing, coaching those who need support and confirming the writing moves. Continue the writing session until most of the class is done. Children who do not finish the writing can put it in their writing folders and return to it during writing workshop.

3. You might have a share session. Have some children sit in the author's chair and read their writing.

4. Consider displaying the writing on a bulletin board along with the books that you collected on hibernation.

Optional Literacy Lessons and Activities Related to the Bear Books

Reviewing Text Types: Book Sort

Create a center with three book bins. Put a selection of fiction and nonfiction books in the center basket. Label the other two baskets fiction and informational. Children's task at the center is to sort each of the books into the correct basket.

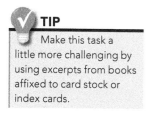

TIP

Make this task a little more challenging by using excerpts from books affixed to card stock or index cards.

Read More Bear Books

If your students like the character Bear, there are seven more Bear books by Karma Wilson to read and enjoy:

- *Bear Feels Scared*
- *Bear Feels Sick*
- *Bear Says Thanks*
- *Bear's Loose Tooth*
- *Bear's New Friend*
- *Bear Stays Up for Christmas*
- *Bear Wants More*

These books are written at approximately text level K, so many second graders will be able to read the books independently or in guided reading groups. You will have to read them aloud to most kindergartners and first graders.

Word Sorts

Bear Snores On is a rhyming book, offering several opportunities to examine spelling patterns in words. Create these word sorts using key words from the book:

- *toe, snow (-oe, -ow)*
- *see, tea (-ee, -ea)*
- *air, share, bear (-air, -are, -ear)*

All Kinds of Bears

Bear appears to be a brown bear, maybe a grizzly bear. Learn more about brown bears, grizzly bears, and other types of bears by reading the following books written at text levels suitable for guided and independent reading for K–2 children:

Book Title	Author	Publisher and Year	Text Level
American Black Bears	Molly Kolpin	Capstone, 2012	K
Brown Bears	Marcia S. Freeman	Capstone, 1999	E
Grizzly Bears	Molly Kolpin	Capstone, 2012	K
Polar Bears	Molly Kolpin	Capstone, 2012	K

Reinforcing Vocabulary with Total Physical Response

Bear Snores On features some rich vocabulary words that represent actions, such as *creep, sneak, peek, slurp, scuttle, flutter, snarl,* and *whimper.* After talking about these words, create two identical sets of word cards containing them. Display one set in a pocket chart. Put the other set of cards face-down on a table. Have one child at a time come up to the table, select a card, read it silently, and then act it out. The other children will guess which word the child is demonstrating.

Comparing Hibernating Animals Chart

Why Do Bears Sleep All Winter? A Book about Hibernation tells about other hibernating animals. Use the information in the book to create a chart comparing the hibernation experiences of bears, desert toads, snakes, Arctic ground squirrels, and wood frogs. For each animal indicate on the chart where it hibernates, how long it hibernates, and any other features of hibernation that you choose to include.

Do Your Own Inquiry

After engaging in the whole class inquiry experience, some children will be eager to do their own inquiries. Children can work alone or in groups. Have children decide on a question and submit it to you. Gather resources to help children find the answers to their question. Schedule a time for children to share what they have learned. Schedule only one or two inquiry shares per day to ensure that children will enjoy them while remaining within their attention limits.

Other Fiction/Informational Paired Book Sets for Inquiry

Below are some paired book sets featuring a fiction book with a question for inquiry and an informational book to answer the question. These choices are based on questions that children have actually asked me after reading the fiction book. Paired book sets that you create from your students' questions make the best choices for your class.

How and Why Do Birds Build Nests?

1. *Who Took the Farmer's Hat?* by Joan Nodset (fiction)

   Farmer Brown has a favorite hat. One day the wind blows it off his head. Farmer Brown searches for it all over the farm. When he finds it, a bird has built a nest inside it. The book is a text level I, making it a good choice for some first grade and second grade guided reading groups.

2. *Mama Built a Little Nest* by Jennifer Ward (informational)

   Would a bird really build a nest inside a hat? This book shows the wide variety of nests that birds build. The book features content-rich sidebars with details about each species and its nest-building habits.

TIP
Mama Built a Little Nest is available in digital format to give children an up-close look at Steve Jenkins' incredible illustrations.

What Is Snow? Why Does It Snow?

1. *Blizzard* by John Rocco (fiction)

   This story was inspired by the author's memories of a blizzard in Rhode Island. In 1978, 53 inches (134.6 centimeters) of snow swallowed up the entire town, transforming the familiar landscapes into something alien and awesome. Mark off the 53-in (134.6-cm) point on a wall or a door so children can see exactly how much snow we are talking about.

2. *The Story of Snow: The Science of Winter's Wonder* by Mark Cassino & Jon Nelson (informational)

   It is unimaginable that a tiny, fragile, delicate snowflake can wreak the havoc of the Rhode Island Blizzard of 1978. This book gives children the in-depth story of snow (e.g., what it is made of and how it forms), and readers can get a close look at this miracle.

TIP
The Story of Snow: The Science of Winter's Wonder is available in digital format.

What Is a Llama?

1. *Is Your Mama a Llama?* by Deborah Guarino (fiction)

   Lloyd the llama asks his animal friends if their mama is a llama. In a riddle reply, each animal gives Lloyd hints about what kind of animal its mother is. Children love the rhyming text and solving the riddles before Lloyd.

2. *Llamas* by Mary R. Dunn (informational)

   Recently llamas have turned up in several popular picture books. So exactly what is a llama? In this book, available as an interactive digital book from Capstone, readers can learn about llamas, including their habitats, diet, stages of development, and how they stay safe.

Why Does the Moon Change Shape?

1. *Kitten's First Full Moon* by Kevin Henkes (fiction)

   In this Caldecott-winning book, Kitten sees a full moon for the first time in her life. She thinks that it's a saucer of milk, so she's determined to get that milk.

2. *The Moon Seems to Change* by Franklyn M. Branley (informational)

   Sometimes the moon looks like a big round ball. That is the moon that Kitten saw. Sometimes it is just a sliver in the sky. Does it really change? What does it do and why? This book is from the renowned and respected "Let's Read and Find Out" series. Children might be inspired to keep a moon journal after reading this book.

What Kinds of Animals Hatch from Eggs?

1. *Duck and Goose* by Tad Hills (fiction)

   Duck and Goose see a large dotted ball. They decide that it is an egg. They argue about who now owns the "egg." Who saw it first? Who touched it first? Eventually, they decide to co-own the "egg" and sit on it, eager to see what will hatch from it.

2. *Guess What Is Growing Inside This Egg?* by Mia Posada (informational)

   The title question leads to a collection of riddles throughout the book about six different living creatures that hatch from eggs. This book makes a great interactive read-aloud and will inspire children to try their hand at riddle writing.

Chapter Six

Reading and Writing: Connecting Fiction and Procedural Texts

One of the challenges faced by competent readers is successfully following written directions. Readers often throw up their hands in frustration after not being able to program their new cell phone successfully, even though they followed the instructions to the letter. Social media are filled with pictures of flat soufflés, crunchy home perms, and all kinds of DIY projects gone wrong. Pinterest has entire pages devoted to this phenomenon.

What makes following written directions so hard? Perhaps it is the vocabulary. Maybe that aspiring chef did not know the difference between whisking, beating, and creaming. In that case, it is not surprising that the soufflé fell. Perhaps it is the specialized equipment required. Maybe that amateur beautician used regular curlers instead of perm curling rods. Under those circumstances, it is no wonder those curls are so brittle and crunchy. Maybe that DIY-er utilized a regular screwdriver instead of a Phillips screwdriver.

Most likely, however, the culprit is the written directions rather than any of the possibilities mentioned above. Good written directions use clear language and a logical sequence. In this anchor lesson, students will read a fun "play rhyme" that chronicles the directions for making the universal American childhood meal, peanut butter and jelly, and an informational book detailing how peanut butter is made. After identifying the qualities of good procedural writing, children will try their own hands at this kind of writing.

Paired Book Anchor Lesson Series #5: Reading and Writing Procedural Texts

Essential Questions

- How can a procedural text help me follow directions?

- How can I write directions that are clear and easy to follow?

Featured Books

Peanut Butter and Jelly: A Play Rhyme

By Nadine Bernard Westcott
E. P. Dutton, 1987
The text of this can't-miss picture book is a play rhyme celebrating the all-time-favorite childhood meal of choice—peanut butter and jelly sandwiches. Westcott's irresistible illustrations include a cast of madcap characters that are sure to delight K–2 children. The last page of the book associates actions with various words that are used in the book and invites the reader to perform the actions as the book is read. It is a boon for kinesthetic learners.

From Peanuts to Peanut Butter

by Kristin Thoennes Keller
Capstone, 2005
Peanut butter does not just magically appear on the grocery store shelf. This classically constructed informational book chronicles the journey from seed to everybody's favorite sandwich spread. The book features color photographs, a table of contents, an index, a glossary, and sidebars. It presents a wonderful opportunity to review and reinforce informational text features.

A. Lessons Using *Peanut Butter and Jelly*

Lesson A-One: Shared Reading of *Peanut Butter and Jelly*

Big book versions of *Peanut Butter and Jelly* are widely available at public libraries, school bookrooms, and online markets. However, new copies are not currently available from the publisher. You can use an LCD projector to create an oversized view of each page on a screen from a standard-sized copy of the book, making it suitable for shared reading.

REMINDER
Remember that some children may be allergic or sensitive to peanuts and may not feel comfortable talking about peanut butter and jelly sandwiches. These lessons can be revised with other procedural texts.

1. Gather children in the large group meeting area. Display the cover of the book so that all children can see it. Read the title and the author's name. Ask, "Who likes peanut butter and jelly?" (show of hands) Then ask, "Who knows how to make a peanut butter and jelly sandwich? Turn and talk to your partner about how it is done."

2. Traditionally, the first reading of a shared reading is done exclusively by you. Children listen, and you read. You might stick to that practice for kindergartners. However, it will be hard to prevent some first and second graders from reading along. So let them! Introduce the first reading of the book by pointing out that they all have a good idea about how peanut butter and jelly sandwiches are made. However, in this book things are done a little differently. Tell them that they will talk about the differences when the reading is over. Read through and enjoy the book, but do not read the final page of the book containing the instructions for the actions. Save it for the next reading.

3. Ask children to think about how they make peanut butter and jelly sandwiches and how the characters in the book made peanut butter and jelly sandwiches. What was the same? What was different? (It is more elaborate—homemade bread, jelly, and peanut butter.) Why do you think the author made it that way? (The author wanted to make the play rhyme last longer and extend the fun.) What about the characters? Why did the author/illustrator choose a baker, elephants, children, a dog, and a cat as characters? (There is a baker because there is homemade bread. There are elephants because elephants like peanuts, and it makes the book funnier. There are children, a dog, and a cat, because they live together in the house.) Look at the mother's reaction on the last three pages. What is she thinking? (The mother is wondering why there are elephants in the house and how much work it will be to clean up the mess.) How is she feeling? (The mother is surprised and angry that she has so much work to do.) What do you think she is saying? (She is probably saying, "Why are there elephants in the house? Why did you make such a big mess? Now you are going to help clean it up!")

Lesson A-Two: Shared Reading of *Peanut Butter and Jelly* with Actions

1. Display the book. Be ready for children's cheers. Do another shared reading of the book.

2. Display the last page of the book. Introduce the actions. Go through the clapping and knee slapping actions for the refrain, "Peanut butter, peanut butter, jelly, jelly." Give children time to practice the actions.

3. Go through the page, reading the text and demonstrating the actions for kneading, baking, slicing, cracking, mashing, spreading, squashing, smearing, and eating. Again, give children time to practice the actions.

4. Read through the book one more time using all of the actions. Be prepared for lots of giggles.

Optional Literacy Lessons and Activities Related to *Peanut Butter and Jelly*

Although these optional lessons are listed here, none of them should intervene between the preceding lesson (A-Two) and the ensuing lesson (B below). There should only be a short transition time between them. The optional lessons appear here only because they logically belong in the section specific to *Peanut Butter and Jelly*, but they should be postponed at least until after the shared procedural writing lesson described in B below.

1. Additional Shared Reading of *Peanut Butter and Jelly*
   The shared reading of a text should take up to five times. For each reading have a different teaching point. Appropriate word study teaching points for this book include the following:
   - consonant blends *gr-* (*grapes*), *gl-* (*globs*), *sm-* (*smear*), *sl-* (*slice*), *cr-* (*crack*)
   - transition words: *first, then, next*
   - words with silent letters: *knead, dough*

2. Peanut Butter and Jelly Vocabulary

The words in *Peanut Butter and Jelly* are perfect for Total Physical Response (TPR). Have children use actions to demonstrate kneading, spreading, glopping, slicing, mashing, and squashing. Recalling the actions from the book will help them. The words can be written in a box, and children can create an appropriate illustration.

3. Retelling Center

Have children retell the *Peanut Butter and Jelly* story as center work. You can provide props, such as toy elephants, toy people, artificial grapes, packing peanuts, etc. Or children can secure images reminiscent of the images in the book and affix them to cardstock to support their retellings.

4. Sequencing Center

Have children use the images from the retelling task and put them in sequential order. You can also have children sequence the steps to making a peanut butter and jelly sandwich. Another option is to provide children with paper folded into six boxes for them to illustrate and write the steps of making the featured sandwich.

5. Listening Center

Put standard-sized copies of *Peanut Butter and Jelly* in the listening center along with an audio recording of the book. You can make your own audio recording if you cannot find an existing one. Children can listen to the recording and read along from the book.

6. Browsing Bin or Lending Library

Books that have been used for shared reading are excellent candidates for the browsing bin or lending library. Support children's fluency development by giving them multiple opportunities to reread *Peanut Butter and Jelly* during independent reading time or at home.

7. *It* Word Book

Words with -*it* in them occur in the story 14 times. Give each child an eight-page booklet with "___-*it*" on each page. Ask children to add a letter on the blank to form a word from the "-*it* word family" (e.g., *sit, hit,* etc.). Then ask children to make an illustration for the new word. Children who are able to can write a sentence to go with the new word.

8. Read More Peanut Butter and Jelly Books

Here are some more peanut butter books that your students might enjoy reading:

- *Peanut Butter & Cupcake!* by Terry Border
- *Peanut Butter and Homework Sandwiches* by Lisa Broadie Cook
- *The Peanut Butter Party* by Jack Roza
- *PB & J Hooray!: Your Sandwich's Amazing Journey from Farm to Table* by Janet Nolan

9. Matching Activity

Have children match phrases from the book with images that depict the phrases (e.g., "Take the dough and knead it.")

B. Shared Procedural Writing for Making a Peanut Butter and Jelly Sandwich

Children have talked about making peanut butter and jelly sandwiches and have read a book about a fun and silly way to make a peanut butter and jelly sandwich. Now the class will engage in some procedural writing on making a peanut butter and jelly sandwich. This activity will serve as a model for another procedural writing task that they will do later in this series of lessons.

TIP
This writing activity can be replaced with writing about making a butter and cheese sandwich for those students who do not eat peanut butter and jelly sandwiches.

1. Tell children that they are going to write the directions for how to make a peanut butter and jelly sandwich. Have them turn and talk about the ingredients and equipment needed. Select pairs of children to share what is on their list. Have other pairs add to the list until it is complete.

2. In full view of children, write the title of the procedure, *How to Make a Peanut Butter and Jelly Sandwich*, on chart paper or on the whiteboard. Make a subheading, *What You Need*. Finally, list the ingredients and equipment. Read each item aloud as you write it, and encourage children to read along. Go back and reread the whole list together when it is completed.

3. Ask children to think about what the first step should be. If you were making a peanut butter and jelly sandwich, what would you do first? Have children talk it over with their partners. Accept answers from several pairs and decide on your first step. It is likely to be, "Get out two slices of bread and put them on a plate."

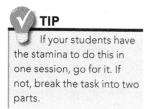

TIP
If your students have the stamina to do this in one session, go for it. If not, break the task into two parts.

4. Decide on the specific language of the first step, and record it on the chart. Repeat the language before you write. Count out the words for younger students or those who require it. Read each word as you write it, and get children to read along. Then go back and reread the sentence when it is completed. Continue in this manner until you have recorded the entire procedure. It is likely to take four steps. Lead children in reading the entire procedure when it is completed.

C. Lessons Using *From Peanuts to Peanut Butter*

Lesson C-One: Interactive Read-Aloud of *From Peanuts to Peanut Butter*

1. Gather children in the large group meeting area. Display the book so that all children can see it. An optimal option for this read-aloud is to use an LCD projector with a standard-sized copy of the book. This will maximize children's ability to see the details of the informational text features. Read the title and the author's name.

2. Read the title page. Review the purpose of the title page. Read the section headings. Pose a few questions to give children practice using the table of contents. (e.g., "Where can we find out how to pick peanuts?")

3. Read through the book, stopping to point out text features, such as sidebars and headings, to discuss the key vocabulary words and to talk about the interesting facts. A world map will help children better understand the fun facts on pages 9 and 14.

4. Finish the book. Have children turn and talk about something they learned about making peanut butter. Select several children to share with the whole group.

Lesson C-Two: Examine the Procedure for Making Peanut Butter

1. Gather children in the large group meeting area. Tell them that they will reread the book to identify the steps for making peanut butter.

2. Read through page 9. Have children turn and talk to identify the first step in making peanut butter. Select some children to share their ideas about the first step. They should say, "Plant peanut plants." Record "Plant peanut plants" on the whiteboard.

3. Return to the book. Read pages 10 and 11. Have children turn and talk to identify the second step in making peanut butter. Select some children to share their ideas about this step. They should say, "Pick the plants." Record "Pick the plants" on the whiteboard.

4. Continue in this manner until you have recorded all of the steps in making peanut butter. When all of the steps are completed, quickly review them. End this session.

5. Create a chart on "How to Make Peanut Butter." Find images to illustrate each step to support children in reading the chart. Engage children in a shared reading of the chart.

Optional Literacy Lessons and Activities Related to *From Peanuts to Peanut Butter*

Here, as in A. Lessons Using *Peanut Butter and Jelly* (beginning on page 73), the optional lessons appear in this location only because they logically belong in the section specific to *From Peanuts to Peanut Butter*. However, the next lesson, D. Procedural Writing (beginning on page 78), should precede any of these optional lessons.

1. George Washington Carver

Page 20 in *From Peanuts to Peanut Butter* introduces George Washington Carver. Here are some grade-appropriate books on Carver to share with your students, especially second graders:

Book Title	Author	Text Level
George Washington Carver	Jo S. Kittinger	H
George Washington Carver	Lynea Bowdish	J
George Washington Carver: The Peanut Scientist	Patricia McKissack and Fredrick McKissack	L

2. Reading More Procedural Texts

Give children more opportunities to read and apply procedural writing with these books:

- *Cardboard* by Daniel Nunn
- *Ed Emberley's Drawing Books* (a whole series!) by Ed Emberley
- *How to Make Bubbles* by Erika Shores
- *Paper* by Daniel Nunn
- *Plastic* by Daniel Nunn

3. More Yummy Procedural Books

- *From Milk to Ice Cream* by Stacy Taus-Bolstad
- *From Seed to Apple Tree* by Steven Anderson
- *From Wheat to Bread* by Stacy Taus-Bolstad
- *Oranges: From Fruit to Juice* by Layne deMarin

4. Video Viewing

View the online video, "The American Peanut Story," from the Virginia Carolinas Peanut website. The Virginia Carolinas Peanut Council also provides information and activities for classroom use. The website is easily located with any search engine.

D. Procedural Writing

1. Display all the procedural charts that were created for this series of lessons (How to Make a Peanut Butter and Jelly Sandwich, How to Make Peanut Butter, Peanut Butter Recipe). You might also include some of the class procedural charts (How to Check Out a Library Book, How to Turn and Talk, etc.). Ask children how these charts help the reader (tell the reader how do something). Have them look at the charts and then turn and talk more specifically about what the charts do to help the reader (give the reader step-by-step instructions). Bring children back together to share their ideas. After they have shared, make sure they understand that good procedural writing starts with a list of what you need and then gives simple and direct action steps in the right order.

2. Brainstorm a list of things that children know how to do and can teach others. Have children discuss in pairs possible candidates for such a list. Then call the pairs together and list their suggestions on the whiteboard. Some of the things that K–2 students can do include feed pets, water plants, set the table, "make" cereal, and play a game. Ask each child to select one thing to write about.

3. Create and give each child a "What You Need" paper, which is simply a list. Circulate and support children in listing the items needed for their procedure. For some classes this will take only one session.

4. Create and give each child a "What You Do" paper. Choose whether children will draw, write, or do a combination of both. Circulate and support children as needed. Most children can complete this task in one session. Give more time as needed.

5. Conduct writing conferences with children. Have them read their procedural writing to you. Find something to praise. Select one item to reteach or reinforce to support the child in his or her understanding about writing.

6. Put children in groups of three or four to share their procedural writing.

Other Fiction and Procedural (or Informational) Paired Book Sets

In most of the paired book sets below, an informational book that contains a procedure is substituted for a procedural book.

The Apple of My Eye

1. *Applesauce Season* by Eden Ross Lipson (fiction)

   An urban child accompanies his grandmother to the farmers' market to buy apples to make applesauce. The book includes a list of apple varieties and, of course, a recipe for making applesauce.

2. *From Apples to Applesauce* by Kristin Thoennes Keller (procedural)

   Unlike the fiction book above, in which the apples start at the farmers' market, this book takes readers to the orchard to observe the apple tree throughout all of its seasons right up until the apples are picked. Like the fiction book, it includes a recipe, so maybe a comparison taste test is in order!

Bubble, Bubble, Toil, and Trouble

1. *Trouble Gum* by Matthew Cordell (fiction)

   It's a rainy day. There's nothing to do. Every time Ruben and Julius begin to have a little fun, their mother tells them that they're too noisy. Then their grandmother gives them bubble gum, and the trouble begins.

2. *Pop! The Invention of Bubble Gum* by Meghan McCarthy (informational)

   In 1928 an accountant at Fleer Gum and Candy comes up with the invention that would delight children for years to come. Maybe you will have to break the school rules and pass out the bubble gum!

Let It Snow!

1. *All You Need for a Snowman* by Alice Schertle (fiction)

   This is a charming, cumulative story of children building a snowman from first falling flakes to outrageous accessories. On each page the "except" tag line encourages predictions and ends with delight and giggles.

2. *Snowballs* by Lois Ehlert (narrative informational)

The book begins with Ehlert's cut paper/collage illustrations of six snow creatures across double-page spreads—a snowman, snow mom, snow boy, snow baby, snow cat, and snow dog. The afterword shows what items "snowman architects" should collect to build these creatures as well as some information about the science of snow.

Color Me Happy

1. *Red: A Crayon's Story* by Michael Hall (fiction)

A blue crayon has been mistakenly labeled "red." Though he tries his best, he just can't make strawberries or hearts. When he plays with his friend Yellow, they can't make an orange. The book opens the door for discussions on self-acceptance and using your strengths.

2. *Wax to Crayons* by Inez Snyder (informational)

So how did the blue crayon get mislabeled as a red crayon? This book might provide some insight. It is an informational book that gives children the inside story of crayon manufacturing. The book includes a glossary, a table of contents, and an index. This book is a text level K, making it suitable for guided and independent reading for many second graders.

On the Road

1. *Are We There Yet, Daddy?* by Virginia Walters (fiction)

Father and son are taking a 100-mile (161-kilometer) road trip to Grandma's house. About every 10 mi (16.1 km), the son wants to know, "Are we there yet, Daddy?" A road map helps the boy understand where they are and how much farther they have to go.

2. *We Need Directions!* by Sarah De Capua (informational)

This Rookie Reader introduces early readers to the world of maps. The book features an index and a picture glossary, well suited for K–2 students. It is written at text level I, making it a good choice for guided reading and/or independent reading for many first and second graders.

Chapter Seven

Reading Across Text Types: Connecting Poetry and Informational Text

Poetry is one of our best allies in supporting students' literacy development. Children in kindergarten through second grade simply cannot resist it. Teachers who recite favorite poems and rhymes to facilitate transitions know that repeated lines, rhyme, and rhythm in poetry provide a strong scaffold for emergent and early readers. The opportunities to review and reinforce phonemic awareness and phonics skills are built right into poems. To a fledgling reader, the abundance of white space on any given page makes it not nearly as intimidating as a full page of print. Repeated reading of poems (and who reads a poem only once?) also contributes to fluency building.

Wolf (2012) calls poetry and nonfiction an "unlikely love affair." Let love bloom in your classroom. The core texts for the lessons in this chapter are a poem for shared reading and an informational picture book for an interactive read-aloud. Hopefully, you will be inspired to assemble more paired book sets of this type using your favorite read-alouds. Of course, some of my favorite poem and picture book paired book sets are included at the end of this chapter.

Paired Book Anchor Lesson Series #6: Losing a Tooth—The Universal Childhood Experience

Essential Question

- How can I use informational texts to learn more about concepts presented in poetry?

Featured Books (Texts)

"My Loose Tooth"

by Ruth Kanarek

The universal childhood experience of losing a tooth is captured in this poem, which describes each step of the journey from first wiggle to tooth fairy reward. It uses a repetitive refrain that kids will not be able to resist. This poem is included in several poetry anthologies and can be located via an online search on either "my loose tooth images" or "my loose tooth kanarek."

What If You Had Animal Teeth!?

by Sandra Markle
Scholastic, 2013

A child has lost his two front teeth and is presented with the question, "What if you had animal teeth!?" The unique attributes of nine different animals' teeth are explored in this book. Each double-page spread has a photograph of an animal displaying its teeth and an illustration of a child with that animal's teeth. Informational text features of the book—sidebars and photographs—are used to convey this fascinating information.

A. Lessons Using "My Loose Tooth"

Lesson A-One: Shared Reading of "My Loose Tooth"

Prepare the poem for shared reading. You can write the poem on a sheet of chart paper, enlarge it to poster size, or project it on a screen. The title and author should be prominently displayed at the top. It is important for children to be able to see the print clearly. You will also want to prepare standard-sized copies to distribute to children. Practice reading the poem out loud before you read it to children.

1. Gather children in the whole group meeting area where the poem has been displayed. Cover the poem, but leave the title visible. Have children turn and talk about their loose tooth experiences. Even children who have not lost a tooth yet can talk about what they think it would be like and their families' traditions around losing teeth. Call children back together and select two children to tell their stories.

2. Tell children that they will read a poem about a loose tooth. Inform them that they will listen to you read it first, and then the class will read it together. Proceed to read the poem aloud to children, actively demonstrating its rhythm.

3. Lead children in reading the poem. Use a pointer to track the words.

4. The child in the poem gets a nickel from the tooth fairy (indicating that it is an old poem). Children will really want to talk about how much money they get from the tooth fairy, so give them a few minutes to turn and talk.

Lesson A-Two: Rereading the Poem for Fluency, Enjoyment, and Skill Instruction

Poems for shared reading can be read five times or even more. Children's increased familiarity with the text will improve the accuracy and fluency of their reading. You can tack on a mini-lesson after each reading—but only one. Start each lesson in this lesson series by rereading the poem. The current lesson (A-Two) features a sample mini-lesson.

1. Call children together in the large group meeting area. Lead them in rereading the poem. You can add movements, such as the ones listed below, to increase student engagement and to provide an additional scaffold to the kinesthetic learners in the class.

   - "wiggly, jiggly tooth": shimmy your shoulders (refrain that occurs three times in the poem)
   - "hanging by a thread": pinch thumb and index finger together, holding them up high, pantomiming to show a long piece of thread
   - "pulled my tooth": pantomime pulling a tooth
   - "put it 'neath my pillow": pantomime putting a tooth under a pillow
   - "went to bed": press palms together, put them next to your head, tilt your head to one side, and close your eyes to pantomime sleeping
   - "fairies took my tooth": flap arms to pantomime flying
   - "now I have a nickel": extend hand palm up to show a coin
   - "and a hole in my head": tap the front of your closed mouth with the index finger

2. After the shared reading of the poem, tell children that one of the things that makes poetry so much fun is the rhyme. If necessary, review the concept of rhyme (words end with the same word chunks) and give some examples that are not in the poem. Reread the poem and ask children to listen for the rhyming words. Have children turn and talk to identify the rhyming words. Select individual children to tell the rhyming words and come to the chart to point them out. Mark the words with highlighter tape or circle them.

3. Point out the two different spelling patterns: *-ed* and *-ead*. Make a list of the *-ed/-ead* rhyming words in two separate columns (one for each ending). Lead children in reading the words in each column.

   Other possible mini-lessons for "My Loose Tooth" include the following:

   - /oo/ as in *loose* and *tooth*, /oo/ (*took*)
   - inflectional endings *-ed* and *-ing* (*pulled, hanging*)
   - changing the *y* to *i* and adding *-es* to make the plural (*fairy, fairies*)
   - figurative language (*hanging by a thread*)
   - consonant sounds /w/ and /j/ (*wiggly, jiggly*)

Lesson A-Three: Identifying the Key Idea from "My Loose Tooth"

1. Conduct a final shared reading of "My Loose Tooth." This time it would be a good idea to select a child to use the pointer and lead the other children in reading the poem.

2. Ask children what the poem teaches us about teeth. Have them turn and talk. Call children back together. Pose the question again. Someone will undoubtedly say, "Teeth come out." Agree and tell children that they will read another book to find out exactly how and why teeth come out and other interesting facts about teeth.

Optional Literacy Lessons and Activities Related to "My Loose Tooth"

TIP

Consider laminating the poem cards so that you will be able to use them again in future school years.

1. ### Poem Cards
   Make copies of "My Loose Tooth" on standard-sized paper. Affix the copies to cardstock. Put the poem cards in a poetry center or the poetry book basket. Encourage children to reread the poem during independent reading time. Children can also put the poem cards in their independent reading book baggies.

2. ### "My Loose Tooth" Illustrated Booklet
   Make children a four-page booklet. The first page of the booklet will be the cover. The cover will have the poem's title and a line of text that says, "Illustrated by _____." The child will fill in the blank with his or her name. The second page will have the first stanza of the poem and a space for an illustration. The third and fourth pages will have the second and third stanzas of the poem respectively along with spaces for illustrations. Children's illustrations will demonstrate their understanding of the poem's text.

3. ### Pocket Chart Sequence
   Write the lines of the poem on sentence strips. Have children arrange the lines of the poem in the correct order in a pocket chart and then read the correctly sequenced poem.

4. ### My Own Loose Tooth Story
   Children will not be able to stop talking about their lost tooth experiences, so have them talk, draw, and write about their own tooth stories. Put them in groups of two or three to talk it over. Then give them paper with a space for drawing and lines for writing.

5. ### Around the World with Tooth Traditions
   In the United States children often put their teeth under their pillows for the tooth fairy to take and leave money. However, different cultures have different customs regarding lost teeth. Share these books with your students:
   - *I Lost My Tooth in Africa* by Penda Diakité
   - *Throw Your Tooth on the Roof: Tooth Traditions Around the World* by Selby Beeler

6. ### Loose Tooth Stories
   Here are some fiction read-alouds about losing teeth:
   - *Arthur's Tooth* by Marc Brown
   - *Little Rabbit's Loose Tooth* by Lucy Bate

7. Read All About Teeth

Here are some informational books about teeth:

- *Caring for Your Teeth* by Sian Smith
- *Open Wide* by Laurie Keller

B. Lessons Using *What If You Had Animal Teeth!?*

Lesson B-One: Interactive Read-Aloud of *What If You Had Animal Teeth!?*

1. Ask children, "What happens after teeth come out?" Someone will tell you that new teeth will grow in. Then read the first page of the book, which ends with the sentence, "But what if an animal's teeth grew instead?" Pause for reaction time.

2. Display the cover of the book. Read the title and the author's name. Return to the first page and reread it. Have children turn and talk to answer the question, "If you grew animal teeth, which animal's teeth would you like to have?" Jot down a quick list of the responses you get. Tell children that they will learn about animal teeth—some that are on the list of their responses and some that are not.

3. Read through the entire book, pausing on individual pages for children to react and respond. Some possibilities include the following:

   - (Page 7) "What is the little girl doing? Why is she so happy?" (The little girl has shark teeth and has lost a lot of teeth at once. She put the teeth under her pillow and is expecting to get a lot of money from the tooth fairy.)
   - (Page 9) "What would you use your tusk for if you were a narwhal?" Let children turn and talk, then share a few answers with the whole group.
   - (Page 19) "Why is the little girl throwing away her toothbrush and toothpaste?" (The little girl has hippopotamus teeth. The top teeth clean the bottom teeth, so she does not need a toothbrush or toothpaste anymore.)

4. Finish the book. Revisit page 30, which explains why human teeth fall out. Talk through the process with children.

Lesson B-Two: Comparing Animal and Human Teeth

Select at least four of the animals from *What If You Had Animal Teeth!?* to create an animal teeth comparison chart. If your students have the stamina, the chart can include all of the animals in the book. Otherwise, pick the animals that received the most enthusiastic responses from your students. The chart should include humans in addition to the selected animals. Create a chart that compares the animals' teeth with respect to size, shape, and number of sets. The chart should also have room to record other interesting facts for each animal. In order to leave your hands free to record the information on the chart, project the pages of the book onto a screen.

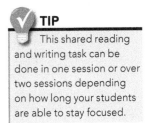

TIP
This shared reading and writing task can be done in one session or over two sessions depending on how long your students are able to stay focused.

1. Tell children that they will make a chart to make it easier to see how animal teeth are similar to and different from our teeth. Lead children in reading the headings of the chart.

2. Reread the name of the first animal on the chart. Go to the page in the book that describes the featured animal's teeth. Tell children to listen carefully to find out the size, shape, and number of sets of that animal's teeth as well as other interesting facts that would be appropriate to put on the chart. Read the page. Then ask children the following questions:

   • What size are the teeth?
   • What shape are the teeth?
   • How many sets of teeth does this animal get?
   • What other interesting facts can you tell about this animal's teeth?

   Select a child to show you where to write the information. Record the information and reread what you have written after each answer is completed.

3. Lead children in a shared reading of the chart when it is completed. You can engage children in a game to review the information on the chart. Use clues, such as "I am thinking of an animal whose teeth can grow to be 10 inches (25.4 centimeters) long."

Lesson B-Three: Writing About Animal Teeth

1. Be sure that the animal teeth comparison chart is displayed where children can see it. Give each child a sheet of writing paper that has space for drawing. Draw a line down the middle to divide the paper in half. Tell children to pick one of the animals from the book, and then give them the following instructions:

   • In the drawing space, draw the animal with its mouth open. Make sure that its teeth can be clearly seen. Make this drawing in the first box.
   • Draw yourself with your mouth open showing your teeth. Make this drawing in the second box.
   • Tell how your teeth and the selected animal's teeth are alike on one side of the paper.
   • Then tell how your teeth and the selected animal's teeth are different on the other side.

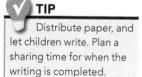

TIP
Distribute paper, and let children write. Plan a sharing time for when the writing is completed.

2. Children have probably been talking about which animal's teeth they would like to have. So capitalize on all of that talk to support some opinion writing. Display your opinion writing anchor chart that you co-created with your students in Chapter Three (see page 46).

Optional Literacy Lessons Related to *What If You Had Animal Teeth!?*

1. ### Teeth Book Text Set

   Read more about animal teeth with the following books:

Book Title	Author	Text Level
A Look at Teeth	Allan Fowler	I
Teeth	Rebecca Rissman	I
The Tooth Book	Dr. Seuss	H
Whose Teeth Are These?	Wayne Lynch	N

2. ### Teeth Sort

   Create images of the animal teeth from the book and affix them to cards. Engage children in an open sort activity. Children may sort the teeth into categories based on any factor they wish (e.g., size, shape, and so on), but they must label the factor and tell why each set of teeth was placed in the correct category. This task can be oral or written.

3. ### Sandra Markle Animal Parts Books
   If your students enjoyed *What If You Had Animal Teeth!?*, then they will probably also enjoy these other offerings by Sandra Markle:
   - *What If You Had Animal Feet!?*
   - *What If You Had Animal Hair!?*

4. ### Which Teeth Would You Use?
   What If You Had Animal Teeth!? told about the interesting attributes of each animal's teeth. Challenge your students to find the perfect teeth for the following tasks:
   - dig a hole
   - chew a cactus
   - lift a log
   - cut down a tree
   - eat an apple

Continuing the "Unlikely Love Affair": Other Paired Book Sets

Below are several more paired book sets with poems and informational texts. They will be sure to delight and inform your students.

The Water Cycle

1. **"The Water Cycle" by Helen H. Moore (poem)**

   This is a charming poem with an A, A, B, B rhyme pattern. It explains the water cycle, jumping from a childish perspective to a somewhat more realistic understanding and then back to a childish perspective. It is included in several poetry anthologies for instructional purposes and can be located via an online search using the title and the author's name.

2. *All the Water in the World* **by George Ella Lyon (informational)**

   With lyrical language and gorgeous illustrations, Lyon follows the path of water. This book highlights the importance of water to all living things and encourages conversation.

Men at Work

1. **"The Cherry Picker" by Hope Vestergaard (poem)**

   The cherry picker is just one of the poems in the book *Digger, Dozer, Dumper.* You can also read poems about an ambulance, a backhoe, a snowplow, and about a dozen more trucks and construction machines. The poems are noisy, rhyming, and rollicking. Read a poem to go with each of the machines that you encounter while reading the informational book on construction that forms the other half of this paired book set.

2. *Construction Zone* **by Cheryl Willis Hudson (informational)**

   This book invites your students into the construction of a building. The names and roles of all the workers and machines are explained—from the architect's plan to the finished building. The complex process is clarified in child-friendly language that is supported by Richard Sobol's breathtaking photographs.

Pandas

1. **"If You Were a Panda Bear" by Wendell and Florence Minor (poem)**

   If You Were a Panda Bear is a gently illustrated picture book containing a series of poems about various types of bears. The first poem in the book, which has the same title as the book itself, highlights the distinguishing features and activities of pandas in rhyme.

2. *Panda Kindergarten* **by Joanne Ryder (informational)**

   The only things that are cuter than pandas are baby pandas. This book documents a day in the life of 16 panda cubs at the Wolong Nature Reserve. The reserve's mission is to conserve and protect China's giant pandas. Readers get to enjoy seeing pictures of the cubs while they climb, play, eat, and nap.

The Knee Bone's Connected to the Leg Bone

1. **"Me and My Skeleton" by Sue LaBella (poem)**

   This rhyming poem describes the purpose of the skeleton. It can be located via an online search using the title and the author's name.

2. ***The Skeleton Inside You* by Phillip Balestrino (informational)**

   This classic informational book explains the function, composition, and structure of the human skeleton.

Animal Movements

1. **"Jump and Jiggle" by Evelyn Beyer (poem)**

   Each line of this poem features two words—an animal's name and how the animal moves. It is great for shared reading and even better for acting out. It can be located via an online search using the title and the author's name.

2. ***Move!* by Steve Jenkins and Robin Page (informational)**

   The first author, who is also a Caldecott Honor-winning illustrator, captures the movement of animals and brings it to your students. The book tells how animals move and why they move that way.

Chapter Eight

Reading and Writing Across Text Types: Two Types of Informational Books

Every second grader will tell you that the author's purpose for writing a nonfiction text is to inform rather than to entertain. Perhaps that is true for the classically constructed informational text, but there is another type of informational text called "narrative nonfiction." Narrative nonfiction is a genre of writing that uses literary styles to share factual information. Gutkind (1997) says that the purpose of nonfiction narratives is "to make nonfiction stories read like fiction, so that your readers are as enthralled by fact as they are by fantasy."

Enthralled by fact! What teacher would pass up that kind of opportunity to enthrall? This paired book set starts off with a rhythmic, rhyming shared reading and finishes with the guided reading of a classically constructed informational text. The books have very similar titles and cover similar content. The books will be read back to back without additional activities and extensions between the readings.

Paired Book Anchor Lesson Series #7: Narrative and Traditional Informational Nonfiction

Essential Questions

- How can I use a classic informational text to enhance and extend the information obtained from a narrative nonfiction text?

- How do children around the world get to school?

Featured Books

This Is the Way We Go to School: A Book About Children Around the World

by Edith Baer

Scholastic, 1990

Children all over the world wake up in the morning and go to school. But how do they get there? This lively, rhyming text transforms your students' concept of school transportation from minivan car pools to skis, cables, and snowmobiles. The couplets are contagious and will soon have children reading along.

This Is the Way We Go to School

by Laine Falk

Children's Press, 2010

Familiar title, eh? Your students are sure to point that out to you. This nonfiction reader addresses the same topic—the way that children go to school around the world. Instead of watercolor illustrations and rhyme, this book uses photographs, an index, a glossary, and captions to show how children go to school.

Me on the Map

by Joan Sweeney

Crown, 1996

This book is a wonderful tool for introducing children to map reading. It starts with a child's room, first presented as a picture, then as a map with the objects in the room represented as symbols. In a concentric pattern, the book continues to the child's street, neighborhood, town, state, country, and finally the world.

A. Lessons Using *This Is the Way We Go to School: A Book About Children Around the World*

Lesson A-One: Shared Reading of *This Is the Way We Go to School: A Book About Children Around the World*

1. Gather children in the large group meeting area. Display the big book on the easel. Read the title, the author's name, and the illustrator's name. Tell children to listen to the book to learn about all the different ways that children go to school.

TIP

If you cannot secure a big book version of the book, use a standard size and project the pages onto a screen.

2. Read aloud the entire book without tracking and without any interruptions so that children can enjoy the rhyme and rhythm of the text and internalize the book's content.

3. Display the last double-page spread of the book showing the world map. Point out where your school is located on the map, and note the different places shown in the book.

4. This book always generates a lot of conversation. Have children turn and talk about how they *would like* to go to school. Select some children to share with the whole class. Do an informal polling to identify the most popular choice for transportation to school.

5. Ask children who walk to school to raise their hands. Then do the same for children who come to school in a car, on a school bus, or on bicycles. Make a chart entitled, "This Is the Way Children Go to School" that lists all the ways documented in the book and in your class.

Lesson A-Two: Rereading of *This Is the Way We Go to School: A Book About Children Around the World* to Increase Student Participation

1. Gather children in the large group meeting area in front of the big book. Tell them that you are going to read the book again, and this time you would like everyone to read along. Tell them that after they are done reading, they will get to talk about some of the different ways children go to school.

2. Read the book using the oral cloze procedure. When you reach the last rhyming word on a double-page spread sequence, pause to elicit children's participation. For example, read "Liz and Larry, as a rule, wear their jogging shoes to school." Then pause after the word *to* so that children can supply the word *school*.

3. Return to several of the particularly interesting pages to discuss the unique forms of transportation, such as the Staten Island Ferry, the cable cars (both in San Francisco and Switzerland), the horse and buggy, the vaporetto, the skis, and the snowmobile. In each case ask children why that mode of transportation is necessary in that particular location.

B. Guided Reading of *This Is the Way We Go to School*

This book is written at text level I. You will have to decide how the book will be read and how many sessions will be needed to read the book. For example:

- Students who can read books at text levels H and I can read the book in a guided reading group (some first graders and most second graders).
- Students who can read books at text level J or higher can read the book independently (many second graders and some first graders).
- You will need to read the book aloud to students who are reading books at text level G or lower.

1. Distribute copies of the book to children. They will immediately notice that the title is the same as the shared reading book. Ask students to recall the different ways children went to school in the other book.

   Direct children's attention to the table of contents on page 3 of the book. Solicit a child to remind the group of the purpose of a table of contents. Ask another child to demonstrate how to use it.

   This book has a bold word in each "chapter." A good strategy lesson for the book is to see how the author uses bold words to help the reader understand an important concept—"the featured vehicle" on each page. Model how to use bold words using page 5. A child will be able to read the word *bus*. Ask children to look on the page to see how the author helps the reader understand what a bus is. Someone will tell you that there is a photograph at the bottom of the page, and the word *bus* is written in red with an arrow pointing to the bus. Tell children that they all knew what a bus was even before looking at the photograph or noting the bold word. But throughout the book, there will be vehicles that are unfamiliar to them, and the bold word and the photograph will help them understand what the vehicle looks like.

2. Tell students to read pages 4 and 5 using the words and illustration to find out how children in the United States go to school. Listen in on one child reading, coaching and confirming strategy use. After students finish reading the pages, talk about the different ways that children go to school in the United States.

3. Tell students to read the next "chapter" through page 11 to find out about the wheeled vehicles that children ride to school. Listen in on two or three children reading, coaching and confirming strategy use. Children might need to be reminded to use the chunking strategy for words like *pedicab* and *underground*. After students finish reading the pages, talk about the different wheeled vehicles that children ride to school.

4. Direct children to the next "chapter" to read about traveling over water and snow. They should read through page 15. Continue coaching and conferring with children. After students finish reading the chapter, talk about why children would need to take boats or snowmobiles to school.

5. Direct children to read the final "chapter" through page 19, which discusses children walking to school or riding animals. This will be your last opportunity to coach readers using this book. When children are done reading, they will be eager to answer the questions posed by the book on pages 16 and 17.

6. Save pages 20 and 21 for a whole class discussion (in Lesson C-Two below). Direct children's attention to pages 22 and 23, the glossary. Tell children that the glossary is like a "private dictionary" for that book. Point out that the words are in alphabetical order, and that the pronunciation aids will help them say the words correctly. Finalize discussion of the book. Tell children that they will revisit this book as a whole class.

C. Lessons Using Both Books

TIP

This task can be completed in one or two sessions, depending on the stamina of your students.

Lesson C-One: Comparing and Contrasting the Two Books

Create a classroom-sized Venn diagram to compare and contrast the two books—*This Is the Way We Go to School: A Book About Children Around the World* and *This Is the Way We Go to School*. Affix an image of each book cover next to one the overlapping circles.

1. Engage children in shared writing to record how the books are alike and how they are different. Select a child to report a likeness or a difference. Ask the child to tell if he or she is going to report on how the books are alike or how the books are different. After the child has reported, record the fact on the Venn diagram, using shared writing. Continue in this manner until the diagram is complete. Be sure to address the basic differences between narrative and informational nonfiction. You might need to ask pointed questions such as, "Which one has a table of contents?" or "Which one is a narrative?"

2. When the chart has been completed, lead children in a shared reading of the Venn diagram. Read each segment—first the unique aspects of one book, then the unique aspects of the other one, and finally how the books are alike.

3. Ask children which book they liked best. Have them turn and talk to a partner about their preference. Distribute paper and have them write about the book they liked best. Remind them to be sure to give a reason. Tell them that they can use the Venn diagram as a resource. You can provide a template as a scaffold.

TIP

There are many templates of Venn diagrams available online.

Lesson C-Two: A Closer Look at Maps

In addition to using the chart that was created from the first book and focusing on two specific pages in the second book, this lesson also entails a read-aloud of a third book.

1. Display the "This Is the Way Children Go to School" chart created at the end of Lesson A-One (see page 92). Recall that the chart contains the methods of transportation mentioned in the first book or used by members of your class. Lead children in a shared reading of the chart. Hold up a copy of the second book, *This Is the Way We Go to School*. Ask children if there are any vehicles in this book that do not appear on the chart. When someone replies, *pedicab*, add it to the chart.

2. Display pages 20 and 21 of the second book on the screen using a projector. Briefly discuss maps and their purpose. Ask a volunteer to read aloud the text on the displayed pages. Select volunteers to match the kids in the photo with the countries that they live in on the map. Quickly point out some of the features of the map, such as the compass rose, the equator, the continents, and the oceans.

3. Read aloud the book *Me on the Map* by Joan Sweeney (1996). It is available in digital format. By projecting the images on the screen, you will enable

students to see the details of the map more clearly. This book will help children to understand maps better.

4. Invite children to make a map. Second graders and some of the first graders who live close to school can map out their route from home to school. Kindergartners and some first graders might make a map of their bedroom or their classroom using the pages of *Me on the Map* as a model. After the maps are completed, divide children into groups of three or four to share.

Optional Literacy Lessons and Activities Related to the *Going to School* Books

Word Families

This Is the Way We Go to School: A Book About Children Around the World is told in rhyme. Select some high-utility word families to use for creating word sorts and word ladders. Such word families that occur in the book include: *-ill (hill)*, *-ow (tow)*, *-ar (car)*, *-ay (bay)*, *-ain (train)*, *-ail (rail)*, *-ing (ring)*, *-oat (boat)*, *-ide (ride)*, and *-ine (line)*. Children can also sort by spelling patterns for the word families *-ain/-ane* and *-ail/-ale*.

Illustrated Class Song Book

This Is the Way We Go to School is also a nursery song. Engage children in singing the song. Write the words of the song on a sheet of white construction paper or cardstock, one verse per page, and have a different child illustrate each page. You can use standard-sized paper or 12-by-18-inch (30.5-by-45.7-centimeter) paper to make a big book. Create new verses about the things that children do in school that are not in the song (e.g., "This is the way we sharpen our pencil" or "This is the way we read a book"). This will allow for additional pages so that each child can have his or her own page to illustrate. Laminate the pages and bind them together to make a book. Put the book in the classroom library for children to read and enjoy.

> **TIP**
> There are several videos of the song *This Is the Way We Go to School* available online.

Back in the Old Days ...

Engage children in collecting data. For homework have them go home and ask their parents and grandparents how they went to school when they were children. Create two graphs—one for the parents and another for the grandparents. Compare the graphs—including the chart created in Lesson A-One about students in your class (see page 92)—to see how going to school has changed over the generations. Follow up this activity by reading *Going to School* by Rebecca Rissman to see other ways that school has changed over the generations. Children can confirm the information in the book with their parents and grandparents.

Schools Around the World

Schools Around the World by Clare Lewis is an informational book that shows what happens in schools around the world once children arrive. This book is written at text level H, making it a good choice for guided reading for first grade.

Shared Reading of *On the Go*

 Engage children in a shared reading of *On the Go* by Ann Morris. A big book version is available in school bookrooms and public libraries. This book looks at the various forms of transportation used around the world. Children can compare the modes of transportation in this book to the modes of transportation used in *This Is the Way We Go to School*.

Other Paired Book Sets Featuring Narrative and Informational Nonfiction

A narrative nonfiction book is a good way to introduce content topics to kindergarten through second grade students. The literary style, rhyme, and rhythm capture their attention. Students listen, and the questions begin. Follow it up with a classic informational book to deepen children's knowledge on the topic. Below are some great pairs.

Turtle Time

1. *One Tiny Turtle* by Nicola Davies (narrative)

   Author Davies tells the story of one sea turtle's life from hatchling to mother who lays her eggs on the beach where she was born. Using lyrical language that must be read aloud, readers learn about the turtle's habitat and lifestyle. The gorgeous illustrations simply mesmerize children.

2. *Sea Turtles* by Laura Marsh (informational)

   This is a classic informational book with photographs, table of contents, captions, sidebars, and a glossary. Readers will learn about various types of sea turtles, where they live, what they eat, and what dangers they face in the oceans.

Behold the Bats

1. *Bat Loves the Night* by Nicola Davies (narrative)

   The sun has set and Bat wakes up. Davies takes readers along for the ride as Bat swoops and soars through the air, searching for food using echolocation, and finally returns home as the sun begins to rise.

2. *Bats: Nocturnal Flyers* by Rebecca Rissman (informational)

   Readers fly through the night with the bats to learn more about these "nocturnal flyers." Readers will learn about what bats eat, where they live, and what they do all night long.

Hail to the Chief

The following two books make a great paired book set for President's Day.

1. *So You Want to Be President?* by Judith St. George (narrative)

   This delightful book looks at the quirks, habits, commonalities, differences, and interesting stories of the men who have served as president of the United States. The book is the recipient of a Caldecott Medal.

2. *What Does the President Do?* by Amanda Miller (informational)

   This nonfiction reader from Scholastic News gives readers a glimpse at how presidents spend their time, which includes giving speeches, making laws, attending meetings, and taking a little time to have some fun. The book has nonfiction text features, including a table of contents, sidebars, and an index.

Man's Best Friend

1. *Tuesday Tucks Me In: The Loyal Bond Between a Soldier and His Service Dog* by Luis Carlos Montalván and Bret Witter (narrative)

   Tuesday the dog tells readers about how he supports the military veteran Luis. Tuesday wakes up Luis in the morning, helps him negotiate the subway and cross busy streets, and guides him back home at the end of the day.

2. *Assistance Dogs* by Mari Schuh (informational)

   This book tells readers how assistance dogs are trained to do jobs, such as turning on lights, picking up keys, and opening doors. This informational book features a table of contents, an index, photographs, and a glossary.

Elephant Seals

1. *Elizabeth, Queen of the Seas* by Lynne Cox (narrative)

   Elizabeth is an elephant seal who somehow finds her way into the Avon River in Christchurch, New Zealand. She charms the residents of that city by sunbathing, waddling in mud, and napping on the grass. Then she starts venturing into traffic, and the residents of Christchurch decide that something must be done.

2. *Elephant Seals* by Megan C. Peterson (informational)

   Get the facts about elephant seals in this informational book, which includes a table of contents, photographs, an index, a glossary, and recommendations for additional resources, including some on the Internet. This book provides details about the life cycle, habitat, and diet of an elephant seal.

Chapter Nine

Reading and Writing Across Texts Written by the Same Author

Anne Tyler has written a book, *A Spool of Blue Thread* (2015), and I am torn. Should I put my name on the reserve list at the public library or bite the bullet and preorder it on Amazon? Tyler is one of my favorite authors. I know that she will very quickly grab my attention, and soon I'll be promising myself that I'll stop reading a chapter to mark student papers or answer my e-mails or start dinner.

You play a key role in helping your students discover favorite authors. When you read aloud and stock classroom libraries with books written by authors who understand the hearts and minds of 5-, 6-, and 7-year-old children, you open the door to the love affair of reading. Once a child has found a favorite author, he or she eagerly looks forward to the next book. That child is willing to persevere when the text becomes a bit of a challenge. The amount of reading done by the child increases, and hence the rate of reading proficiency increases. After all, that's the goal, isn't it?

As the title of this book tells us, two books are better than one. However, when looking at books written by the same author, three or four books are even better than two. These lessons feature the work of Australian author Mem Fox. Fox has written over 30 books for K–2 students. Many of her books are written at text levels that are accessible for K–2 readers. Therefore, her books can be used for interactive read-aloud, shared reading, guided reading, and independent reading. The books selected for these lessons will work well for most kindergarten and first grade classrooms. Options for more challenging books will also be recommended.

Paired Book Anchor Lesson Series #8: Going Down Under with Mem

Essential Question

- How does reading a book by a certain author help me read other books by that same author?

Featured Books

Hattie and the Fox

by Mem Fox
Bradbury Press, 1986

Hattie and her farmyard friends are enjoying a nice day in the sun, when Hattie notices something suspicious in the bushes. The repetition, drama, and suspense result in a thoroughly engaging and enjoyable read-aloud or shared reading experience.

Where Is the Green Sheep?

by Mem Fox
Harcourt, 2004

Cute, colorful sheep frolic and cavort throughout this book. But where is the green sheep? This book is the recipient of numerous awards, including *Child Magazine* Best Book of the Year 2004, Hornbook Fanfare Best Book, and ALA Notable Book.

A. Lessons Using *Hattie and the Fox*

Lesson A-One: Shared Reading of *Hattie and the Fox*

Big book versions of *Hattie and the Fox* are widely available in school bookrooms, public libraries, and online markets. If you are not able to secure a big book, use a standard-sized copy and project the pages onto a screen using a projector.

1. Gather children in the large group meeting area, where you have displayed the big book version of *Hattie and the Fox* on the easel. Read the title and the author's name. Get a volunteer to name the setting of the story and tell what makes him or her think that the story takes place on a farm. Ask, "Does a fox belong on a farm? Why or why not?" You might say, "A fox on a farm could be a big problem. Let's read to find out what happens."

2. Read the book all the way through without tracking. Also limit conversations and questions. You want children to concentrate on the story content. They will undoubtedly begin reading along once they learn the repetitive refrains of the book.

3. Ask children, "Who do you think the hero was in this story? Why do think that?" Have them turn and talk. Call them back together to share their responses with the whole group. Some children will think that Hattie was the hero because she warned everyone from the very beginning that there was a fox in the bushes. Some children will say that the cow was the hero because she chased the fox away.

Lesson A-Two: Rereading of *Hattie and the Fox* to Increase Student Participation

1. Gather children in the large group meeting area in front of the big book version of *Hattie and the Fox*. Tell them that they will read the book again. This time everyone should read along. Turn to the eighth page past the title page, where all of the animals' replies to Hattie's warnings are listed on a single page. Quickly review all the animals' tag lines. Ask, "What did the pig say?" Follow up with the same question about the horse, the cow, etc. Tell children that you will be listening to hear everyone read these lines when they get to them in the book.

2. Read through the entire book. Use oral cloze when the animals respond to Hattie in order to encourage children to chime in.

   This is technically the end of the lesson from the perspective of increasing student participation. Steps 3–4 of this lesson (which follow immediately below) represent a specific implementation of the fluency and skill instruction described in the next lesson (A-Three). These steps are included here mainly as a step-by-step demonstration for that lesson. Of course if time permits, it is desirable to carry out all four steps in a single lesson so that a single rereading of the book serves both to increase student participation and to provide fluency and skill instruction.

3. Return to the eighth page after the title page. Point out the exclamation point in the sentence "'Good grief!' said the goose." Ask a student to name the punctuation mark and tell what it means. Reiterate that exclamation points convey strong emotions. Authors use it to show that the character is happy, angry, or excited. Ask, "How do you think the goose is feeling?" Have children turn and talk, and then select one or two pairs to share out their responses.

4. Tell children that they can use exclamation points in their writing to show strong feelings, such as happiness, anger, or excitement. Here are two resources for additional lessons on the exclamation point:

   • *Exclamation Mark* by Amy Krouse Rosenthal (2013)
   • "Interjections!" is a musical video by Schoolhouse Rock. Search for it on YouTube. Watch the video prior to showing it to children to ensure that it will be appropriate for your classroom.

Lesson A-Three: Rereading of *Hattie and the Fox* for Fluency and Skill Instruction

Big books can be read three to five times. Be sure to have discussions about the important ideas of the book, including the following:

• Why didn't the animals listen to Hattie until it was almost too late? (They didn't believe her.)
• Do you think Hattie knew there was a fox in the bushes from the very beginning? Why or why not? (Opinions will vary.)
• Do you think the other animals learned a lesson that day? What lesson did they learn? What will they do differently next time? (The animals learned

a lesson. They learned that they should pay attention when someone gives them a warning. The next time they will pay attention.)

Here are some suggestions for focus lessons to accompany each rereading:

- exclamation points (see implementation in steps 3–4 of Lesson A-Two above)
- question marks
- quotation marks
- appropriate intonation in oral reading of sentences ending with question marks and exclamation points
- robust vocabulary word (e.g., *frightened*)
- high-frequency word (e.g., *said*)
- character traits of Hattie, fox, goose, pig, sheep, horse, cow

Optional Literacy Lessons and Activities Related to *Hattie and the Fox*

1. ### Pocket Chart Match: Who Said That?
   Match images of the animals in *Hattie and the Fox* with their tag lines.

2. ### Sequence Activity: The Emergence of the Fox
   On the first, fourth, sixth, eighth, and tenth double pages after the title page, Hattie makes five different statements of the form, "I can see _____ in the bushes." Write these statements on sentence strips, in each case filling in the blank space with only the new thing that Hattie sees. For example, when she sees a nose and two eyes, write just "two eyes" in the blank space because Hattie had already seen the nose previously. You can add illustrations as an additional scaffold. Have children put the statements in chronological order.

   > **TIP**
   > This can be done in a pocket chart as a center activity or as a cut-and-paste individual activity.

3. ### Short e and Short o Sort
   Create a picture sort or a word sort with short *e* and short *o* words. Use *hen* and *fox* as guiding words.

4. ### Word Ladder: Change *hen* into *fox*
   This task can be done as a whole group activity, small group activity, or individual activity. The bottom rung of the ladder is *hen*:
   - Change one letter to make *hen, pen.*
   - Change one letter to make *pen, pet.*
   - Change one letter to make *pet, pit.*
   - Change one letter to make *pit, sit.*
   - Change one letter to make *sit, six.*
   - Change one letter to make *six, fix.*
   - Change one letter to make *fix, fox.*

5. ### Readers' Theater

   Hattie and the Fox is the perfect book for readers' theater. No scripts are needed! Give each performer a standard-sized copy of the book. Select a strong reader to be the narrator. Since there are parts for six other performers, put children into groups of seven to practice. After sufficient practice time, let one group per day perform until all the groups have presented.

6. Torn Tissue Collages

Patricia Mullins made the gorgeous illustrations in *Hattie and Fox* using torn tissue paper. Engage children in preparing for the art project by tearing sheets of tissue paper. Give each student a 9-by-12-inch (22.9-by-30.5-centimeter) sheet of manila paper and a small bottle of school glue to create his or her masterpiece. This task will make a good center activity.

B. Lessons Using *Where Is the Green Sheep?*

Lesson B-One: Guided Reading of *Where Is the Green Sheep?*

Where Is the Green Sheep? is written at text level E. If you have students reading books at text levels D–F, this book would make an appropriate choice for guided reading. Lesson C-One below contains a list of Mem Fox books written at higher text levels that are suitable for read-aloud, shared reading, or guided reading in kindergarten through second grade.

1. Assemble a group of four to six children capable of reading books written at text level E. Hold up the book *Where Is the Green Sheep?* Lead them in reading the title of the book, which they should be able to do with relative ease. Point to the author's name and point out that this book is also written by Mem Fox.

2. Level E readers are ready to move beyond an overreliance on picture clues and focus more on print. Model this strategy using the fourteenth page past the title page, which contains the phrase *clown sheep*. Cover the word *clown* with correction tape. Read the sentence aloud, pausing or substituting *blank* for the omitted word. Ask children to look at the illustration and to think of a word that would make sense. They will probably say *juggling*. Congratulate them on their good thinking, confirming that *juggling* would make sense. However, tell them that readers must pay careful attention to the written words rather than relying on pictures. Uncover the word *clown*. Reread the sentence with the omitted word. Tell children that when they read today, illustrations might be useful, but careful readers make sure to use the words that actually appear in writing.

3. Distribute copies of the book to each child. Lead them in reading the title again. Ask them where the green sheep might be. Honor their responses. Tell children to read the book to find out where the green sheep is.

4. While children are reading, conduct individual conferences. Confirm children's correct use of strategies, and coach those who need support. Be sure to record anecdotal notes on your interactions with children to inform future lessons.

5. When every child has finished reading the entire book, call the group back together. Give children an opportunity to share their favorite passage in the book. Talk about the green sheep missing all the fun and why he might be asleep.

6. Lead children in a brief word study exercise with *-ee* words. Write *-ee* on the whiteboard. Have them produce the sound that *-ee* makes. Add letters to the beginning and end of *-ee* to make words. Have children read the words.

Some words that you can use in this exercise include *beet, deep, feet, heel, keep, meet, peel, queen, teen,* and *wheel.*

7. The language is so delightful in this book that it warrants a joyful shared reading. Read the book one more time together, emphasizing the repetitive refrain, "Where is the green sheep?"

Optional Literacy Lessons and Activities Related to *Where Is the Green Sheep?*

1. Word Sort with *e* Words

Give children a set of cards with short *e* words (*hen, red, ten, nest, bet, men*), long *e* words spelled with a single *e* (*be, me, he, she, we*), and long *e* words spelled with a double *e* (*green, sheep, feet, keep, queen*). Have children sort the words. This activity can be adapted by making it a picture sort. You can even make it more challenging by using words such as *squeeze, creek, speech, freeze, street, bleed, screen,* and *cheek.*

2. Make Your Own Green Sheep Caption Book

Give children booklets with four to six pages containing the text, "Here is the _____ sheep." Orally share ideas and encourage creativity (e.g., "Here is the rainbow sheep," "Here is the teeny-tiny sheep," or "Here is the ninja sheep.") Children will fill in the blank to complete the sentence and make an illustration to go with the sentence. Give them a chance to share their caption books in small groups.

3. Pocket Chart

Write descriptive phrases from the book on sentence strips (*red sheep, clown sheep,* etc.). Find matching images to affix to the cards. Have children match the phrases with the corresponding images.

4. Identifying Antonyms

Where Is the Green Sheep? presents a wonderful opportunity to introduce children to antonyms. Explain that "antonyms" are words that have opposite meanings. Then provide plenty of examples, such as *big/little, hot/cold, in/out, wet/dry.* When children begin to catch on, say the word and, using oral cloze, let children provide the antonym. For example:

- *happy* and _____
- *long* and _____
- *open* and _____
- *front* and _____
- *hello* and _____

Engage children in a shared reading of *Where Is the Green Sheep?* by projecting the book pages onto a screen. When each pair of sheep is introduced, children will give a thumbs-up if they are antonyms and a thumbs-down if they are not.

> **TIP**
> This activity can be extended to a pocket chart task that engages children in matching the antonyms that describe a sheep (e.g., *thin sheep/wide sheep, up sheep/down sheep, scared sheep/brave sheep,* and so on).

5. Green Sheep's Adventure Video

Penguin Books Australia made a cute video of the green sheep looking for Mem Fox. You might like to show it to children. You can find it by searching for "The Green Sheep's Adventure" on YouTube. There are several other videos of *Where Is the Green Sheep?* on YouTube, and one of them highlights the words as they are read. You can find this video by searching for "Green Sheep Complete" on YouTube.

C. Exposing Your Students to Other Mem Fox Books

Lesson C-One: The Work of Mem Fox

Lori's students were surprised to learn that *City Dog, Country Frog* was a book by Mo Willems because it was not like his other books. Mo Willems' books are usually funny, and this book was sad. They knew this because they had read, talked about, and enjoyed many of Mo Willems' books and were very familiar with his style.

To help children become familiar more with Mem Fox's style, they will need to read and/or listen to more than two books. Read aloud at least two more Mem Fox books during your daily read-aloud. Then begin the discussion about the work of Mem Fox. Be sure to read aloud *Possum Magic* because this book will introduce students to Australia. Collect as many of Mem Fox's books as you can. Make a display containing the books, a picture of Mem Fox, and the attribute chart that you will create during this lesson. In addition to *Possum Magic*, here are some other Mem Fox books that are suitable for read-aloud, shared reading, or guided reading in kindergarten through second grade:

Book Title	Text Level
Hunwick's Egg	L
Koala Lou	K
The Magic Hat	J
Whoever You Are	I
Zoo-Looking	G

TIP

As an extension activity, you can show children where the author's home country of Australia is located on a world map and its distance from where your students live.

1. ## Mem Fox's Website

   Show children Mem Fox's website (www.memfox.com). Read her "extremely brief bio" to children, and have them listen to Mem read aloud one of her books. Better yet, let children watch a video of Mem reading the book *Hello Baby!* You can find it by searching for "Mem Fox Reads from Hello Baby!" on YouTube. Of course, you will be sure to have a copy of the book available.

2. ## Mem Fox Books Attribute Chart

   Create a Mem Fox Books Attribute Chart on a large piece of butcher paper or bulletin board paper. Make a grid with the following heading at the top of the columns: Title, Characters, Setting, Problem, and Solution.

   The rows will be the individual books (e.g., *Hattie and the Fox, Where Is the Green Sheep, Possum Magic, Koala Lou,* and so on). You might represent the books by using images of their covers.

   As each book is completed, lead children in shared writing to fill in the information on the grid. After the information about a given book has been filled in, use shared reading to read the information. When the chart is completed, use shared reading to read the whole chart together. Then, using the information from the chart, have a discussion about Mem Fox's style. Some questions that might stimulate the discussion include the following:

- What do you notice about Mem Fox's books?
- How are Mem Fox's books alike?
- What do you notice about the characters?
- Where do most of the stories take place?
- How do the characters solve their problems?

By reading more of Mem Fox's books, children will notice that they often feature animals as characters, have rhyming text, and are set in Australia. Several of them are about going to bed.

Lesson C-Two: Writing Connected to Mem Fox's Books

1. Dear Mem …

The classic activity for ending an author study is to write a letter to the author. Mem Fox has published a book that includes some of the letters that she has received from children. It is entitled, *Dear Mem Fox, I Have Read All of Your Books Even the Pathetic Ones: And Other Incidents in the Life of a Children's Book Author.* Select one of the letters from the book, and read it aloud to children. Have children turn and talk about what they would say to Mem Fox and what questions they would ask her in a letter.

Review the friendly letter format (greeting, body, closing) with children. Display a letter writing anchor chart if you have one. Pair up children. Then have them talk through the entire letter using "letter language." If necessary you can give children a friendly letter template as a scaffold. Encourage younger children and emergent writers to include pictures and labels to communicate their messages fully. Circulate while children are writing. Periodically pause the writing to comment on effective strategies that children are using.

When the writing is completed, divide children into groups of three or four to share their letters. You might consider actually mailing the letters to Mem. The mailing address is supplied on Mem Fox's website.

2. Opinion Writing

After reading four or more Mem Fox books, children are likely to have developed a favorite book. Display your opinion writing anchor chart from Chapter Three (see page 46). Pair children up to talk and then write about their favorite Mem Fox books. Tell them that each child should provide reasons why he or she likes a favorite book more than the others. Distribute appropriate paper for this task. Provide an opportunity for children to share.

TIP

Consider compiling the results of this activity and tabulating exactly what the appeal was of the individual books.

3. Informative Explanatory Writing

Australian animals are prominently featured in Mem Fox's books. Extend an invitation to learn more about Australian animals.

Provide resources for children to read about the bandicoot, koala, kangaroo, kookaburra, and wombat. The following books will be helpful:

- *Bandicoots* by Lyn Sirota
- *Kangaroos and Their Joeys* by Anne Giulieri
- *Koalas* by Sara Louise Kras
- *Kookaburra* by Lynn Salem and Josie Stewart
- *Wombats* by Sara Louise Kras

Use the lesson structure in Chapter Five to support children in informative explanatory writing about these animals. Arrange opportunities for children to share their writing with others.

Other Paired Book Sets by Favorite Authors

When looking for authors to use in K–2 classrooms, find ones with the following qualities:

- prolific—the author has written more than 10 books
- diverse readability—books are written at a variety of levels appropriate for read-alouds, shared reading, guided reading, and independent reading
- kid appeal—the author writes books that kids will love
- clever use of language—books include rhyme, humor, and/or robust words
- fabulous illustrations—books include illustrations that engage children and add to the text

The following recommended authors fit these criteria. Remember to share other examples of the author's work with children.

Lois Ehlert

Lois Ehlert is an author/illustrator known for her brightly colored cut paper and collage illustrations. Her books are easy to pair because her work has prevalent themes that include gardens, cats, leaves, colors, and folktales. Gardens are the theme of the books featured here.

1. *Waiting for Wings* (shared reading)

   Children in this book have a butterfly garden and carefully observe the stages of the butterfly life cycle.

2. *Planting a Rainbow* (guided reading)

   A young child watches the growth and development of flowers in rainbow colors from seed or bulb to full bloom.

3. *Growing Vegetable Soup* (guided reading)

   If you want to make the garden pair a trio, you will be able to present flower gardens, vegetable gardens, and butterfly gardens.

Donald Crews

Donald Crews is an award-winning author/illustrator of many informational books for K–2 readers. Crews is the go-to author if you are teaching a transportation unit.

1. *Freight Train* (guided reading)

   All of the cars of a freight train are presented in glorious color and named. This book is a Caldecott Honor book.

2. *Harbor* (shared reading)

   This book captures all the action at the harbor. Names and purposes of the ships, boats, and machines will inform and delight children.

Ezra Jack Keats

Mr. Keats is a Caldecott Award-winning author/illustrator. His books feature diverse urban recurring characters. The Keats characters are also featured in a set of early readers appropriate for guided reading.

1. *The Snowy Day* (read-aloud)

   This is the classic Caldecott Award-winning book about Peter's delight in the first snowfall of the winter. Peter engages in all the things that children do when they play in the snow.

2. *Peter's Chair* (read-aloud)

   Peter is now a big brother. His new baby sister is taking all of Peter's mother's time and attention. His mother wants to take Peter's little chair, paint it pink, and give it to his sister. Even though it is too small for Peter, he is not sure that he wants to let it go. Other books featuring Peter are *A Whistle for Willie* and *Goggles!*

Keiko Kasza

Keiko Kasza is an author/illustrator who writes clever and humorous books, often with a surprise ending. Her characters are usually animals. These books are appropriate for read-alouds in most kindergarten and first grade classrooms and can be used for guided reading for some second graders.

1. *The Wolf's Chicken Stew* (read-aloud)

   The wolf's favorite food is chicken stew. He spies a chicken that would make a great stew, except she's a little thin. The wolf decides to bake and leave some goodies by her house in order to fatten her up.

2. *My Lucky Day* (read-aloud)

   A hungry fox answers a knock at his door one day, and discovers a lost little piglet that has apparently knocked on his door by accident. The fox thinks that it's his lucky day. Is it really?

Jane Yolen

Jane Yolen is an award-winning author who has written more than 300 books in a variety of genres, including chapter books, illustrated fiction, series books, and, of course, picture books that are just right for our K–2 readers. But Jane Yolen is not exclusively an author of books for K–2 readers. When these readers grow and develop, there will still be Jan Yolen books that they can read.

1. *How Do Dinosaurs Say Good Night?* (shared reading)

   This is a bedtime guidebook featuring *Tyrannosaurus rex*, *Triceratops*, and *Pteranodon*. Children are sure to recognize their own bedtime antics in this book. There are more than a dozen "How Do Dinosaurs" books to address all sorts of issues and protocols. Consider using them to make a class version on a topic of children's choosing.

2. *Creepy Monsters, Sleepy Monsters: A Lullaby* (guided reading)

   This is a great shared reading or guided reading book about monsters' bedtimes. It's fun to compare them with the dinosaurs' bedtimes. There is a companion book for this one, entitled *Romping Monsters, Stomping Monsters*.

Final Thoughts on Pairing Texts

You might think that you have reached the end of the book. However, it is only the beginning of your paired book adventure. The next steps are up to you. There are over 20,000 children's books published each year (Barr & Harbison, 2011). There is certainly a perfect book out there, perhaps the latest Caldecott winner, to pair up with your favorite read-aloud or the "launch book" for your upcoming unit of study. To find just the right candidate, seek out a book with the same theme, by the same author, with the same central message, with the same structure, or with a different perspective on the same story.

With the large volume of books available, you are going to need a little help. The following are some screening resources that highlight some of the best books out there.

Capstone

Capstone Publishers has a fine selection of read-alouds, shared reading, independent texts, digital texts, and a guided reading program. Engage Literacy is a comprehensive literacy program for the primary grades that can be used with an individual, small group, or whole class focus. Most of the titles in the Engage Literacy program are provided as fiction and nonfiction pairs. Search for your topic using the online catalog and you are sure to find the perfect book to pair with your featured book.

Horn Book Magazine

Horn Book Magazine is a publication exclusively about children's books. It has both print and online editions as well as a free website containing highlights from the magazine. Each year, *Horn Book* publishes a "Fanfare" list of their choices for the best children's books of the year. All of these lists, for the current year and previous years, are available on their free website (http://www.hbook.com), which also has sections on "choosing books" and "using books" that can aid your search for a book to pair up with the one you plan to use next in your classroom. The full magazine can be accessed in most public and university libraries without paying for a subscription.

Book Links

Isn't this the perfect name for a publication to help you find paired book sets? *Book Links* is a quarterly publication of *Booklist* magazine, published by the American Library Association. Each issue has a theme, making it a great place to look for books on a selected theme. You can access back issues of *Book Links* for free at http://www.ala.org/offices/publishing/booklist/booklinks.

Children's Choice Awards

Children's Choice Awards is a collaborative effort of the International Literacy Association and the Children's Book Council. It is one of the few awards where children select the winners, which can be found at: http://www.cbcbooks.org/childrens-choices.

Children's Literature Blogs

Children's Literature Blogs is another resource worth exploring. Here are a few of my favorites:

- Fuse #8   http://blogs.slj.com/afuse8production
- Book-A-Day Almanac   http://childrensbookalmanac.com
- Watch. Connect. Read.   http://mrschureads.blogspot.com

Independent Bookstores

Another good source for finding books is your local independent bookstore. Independent bookstores do not have to staff hundreds of staff positions like a big chain, so they can be a little more selective. As a result independent bookstores usually attract employees who are real book lovers. They know about the books because they have read them. Your local independent bookstore staff can be very helpful in identifying a book that can transform your chosen book into a paired book set. Make it a practice to visit your local independent bookstore every month and read all of the books newly on display. Luckily, picture books have only about 32 pages, so you can read all of the newly displayed books in just a couple of hours.

Teacher Conferences

Finally, don't overlook teacher conferences as a source for books for your classroom lessons. Every single teacher conference that I have ever attended—local, state, national, and international—has had at least one session on the best children's books. Don't miss it. The room is usually filled to capacity for children's book session, so go to the preceding session to ensure that you get a good seat. The handouts for the session identify all the books that will be discussed during the session and contain brief descriptions of most of them. You'll leave the conference with great ideas for paired book sets. At national teacher conferences, where some copies of the books that are highlighted in the session are often given away, you might even leave with a new book as well.

***

Each reading experience functions as a mentor for the reader's future reading and writing experiences. Don't miss the opportunity to capitalize on your students' reading and writing experiences via paired book sets.

Common Core State Standards Correlation Chart

Common Core State Standards	Ch. 1	Ch. 2	Ch. 3	Ch. 4	Ch. 5	Ch. 6	Ch. 7	Ch. 8	Ch. 9
CCSS.ELA-LITERACY.RL.K.1 With prompting and support, ask and answer questions about key details in a text.									
CCSS.ELA-LITERACY.RL.1.1 Ask and answer questions about key details in a text.									
CCSS.ELA-LITERACY.RL.2.1 Ask and answer such questions as *who, what, where, when, why,* and *how* to demonstrate understanding of key details in a text.									
CCSS.ELA-LITERACY.RL.K.2 With prompting and support, retell familiar stories, including key details.									
CCSS.ELA-LITERACY.RL.1.2 Retell stories, including key details, and demonstrate understanding of their central message or lesson.									
CCSS.ELA-LITERACY.RL.2.2 Recount stories, including fables and folktales from diverse cultures, and determine their central message, lesson, or moral.									
CCSS.ELA-LITERACY.RL.K.3 With prompting and support, identify characters, settings, and major events in a story.									
CCSS.ELA-LITERACY.RL.1.3 Describe characters, settings, and major events in a story, using key details.									
CCSS.ELA-LITERACY.RL.2.3 Describe how characters in a story respond to major events and challenges.									
CCSS.ELA-LITERACY.RL.1.4 Identify words and phrases in stories or poems that suggest feelings or appeal to the senses.									
CCSS.ELA-LITERACY.RL.2.4 Describe how words and phrases (e.g., regular beats, alliteration, rhymes, repeated lines) supply rhythm and meaning in a story, poem, or song.									
CCSS.ELA-LITERACY.RL.K.5 Recognize common types of texts (e.g., storybooks, poems).									
CCSS.ELA-LITERACY.RL.1.5 Know and use various text features (e.g., headings, tables of contents, glossaries, electronic menus, icons) to locate key facts or information in a text.									
CCSS.ELA-LITERACY.RL.K.6 With prompting and support, name the author and illustrator of a story and define the role of each in telling the story.									
CCSS.ELA-LITERACY.RL.1.6 Identify who is telling the story at various points in a text.									

Common Core State Standards	Ch. 1	Ch. 2	Ch. 3	Ch. 4	Ch. 5	Ch. 6	Ch. 7	Ch. 8	Ch. 9
CCSS.ELA-LITERACY.RL.2.6 Acknowledge differences in the points of view of characters, including by speaking in a different voice for each character when reading dialogue aloud.									
CCSS.ELA-LITERACY.RL.K.7 With prompting and support, describe the relationship between illustrations and the story in which they appear (e.g., what moment in a story an illustration depicts).									
CCSS.ELA-LITERACY.RL.1.7 Use illustrations and details in a story to describe its characters, setting, or events.									
CCSS.ELA-LITERACY.RL.2.7 Use information gained from the illustrations and words in a print or digital text to demonstrate understanding of its characters, setting, or plot.									
CCSS.ELA-LITERACY.RL.K.9 With prompting and support, compare and contrast the adventures and experiences of characters in familiar stories.									
CCSS.ELA-LITERACY.RL.1.9 Compare and contrast the adventures and experiences of characters in stories.									
CCSS.ELA-LITERACY.RL.2.9 Compare and contrast two or more versions of the same story (e.g., Cinderella stories) by different authors or from different cultures.									
CCSS.ELA-LITERACY.RL.K.10 Actively engage in group reading activities with purpose and understanding.									
CCSS.ELA-LITERACY.RL.1.10 With prompting and support, read prose and poetry of appropriate complexity for grade 1.									
CCSS.ELA-LITERACY.RL.2.10 By the end of the year, read and comprehend literature, including stories and poetry, in the grades 2–3 text complexity band proficiently, with scaffolding as needed at the high end of the range.									
CCSS.ELA-LITERACY.RI.K.1 With prompting and support, ask and answer questions about key details in a text.									
CCSS.ELA-LITERACY.RI.1.1 Ask and answer questions about key details in a text.									
CCSS.ELA-LITERACY.RI.K.3 With prompting and support, describe the connection between two individuals, events, ideas, or pieces of information in a text.									
CCSS.ELA-LITERACY.RI.1.3 Describe the connection between two individuals, events, ideas, or pieces of information in a text.									

Common Core State Standards	Ch. 1	Ch. 2	Ch. 3	Ch. 4	Ch. 5	Ch. 6	Ch. 7	Ch. 8	Ch. 9
CCSS.ELA-LITERACY.RI.2.3 Describe the connection between a series of historical events, scientific ideas or concepts, or steps in technical procedures in a text.									
CCSS.ELA-LITERACY.RI.1.5 Know and use various text features (e.g., headings, tables of contents, glossaries, electronic menus, icons) to locate key facts or information in a text.									
CCSS.ELA-LITERACY.RI.2.5 Know and use various text features (e.g., captions, bold print, subheadings, glossaries, indexes, electronic menus, icons) to locate key facts or information in a text efficiently.									
CCSS.ELA-LITERACY.RI.2.6 Identify the main purpose of a text, including what the author wants to answer, explain, or describe.									
CCSS.ELA-LITERACY.RI.2.7 Explain how specific images (e.g., a diagram showing how a machine works) contribute to and clarify a text.									
CCSS.ELA-LITERACY.RI.K.9 With prompting and support, identify basic similarities in and differences between two texts on the same topic (e.g., in illustrations, descriptions, or procedures).									
CCSS.ELA-LITERACY.RI.1.9 Identify basic similarities in and differences between two texts on the same topic (e.g., in illustrations, descriptions, or procedures).									
CCSS.ELA-LITERACY.RI.2.9 Compare and contrast the most important points presented by two texts on the same topic.									
CCSS.ELA-LITERACY.RI.K.10 Actively engage in group reading activities with purpose and understanding.									
CCSS.ELA-LITERACY.RI.1.10 With prompting and support, read informational texts appropriately complex for grade 1.									
CCSS.ELA-LITERACY.RI.2.10 By the end of year, read and comprehend informational texts, including history/social studies, science, and technical texts, in the grades 2–3 text complexity band proficiently, with scaffolding as needed at the high end of the range.									
CCSS.ELA-LITERACY.L.K.1.f Produce and expand complete sentences in shared language activities.									
CCSS.ELA-LITERACY.L.1.6 Use words and phrases acquired through conversations, reading and being read to, and responding to texts, including using frequently occurring conjunctions to signal simple relationships (e.g., *because*).									

Common Core State Standards	Ch. 1	Ch. 2	Ch. 3	Ch. 4	Ch. 5	Ch. 6	Ch. 7	Ch. 8	Ch. 9
CCSS.ELA-LITERACY.L.2.6 Use words and phrases acquired through conversations, reading and being read to, and responding to texts, including using adjectives and adverbs to describe (e.g., *When other kids are happy that makes me happy*).									
CCSS.ELA-LITERACY.SL.K.1 Participate in collaborative conversations with diverse partners about *kindergarten topics and texts* with peers and adults in small and larger groups.									
CCSS.ELA-LITERACY.SL.1.1 Participate in collaborative conversations with diverse partners about *grade 1 topics and texts* with peers and adults in small and larger groups.									
CCSS.ELA-LITERACY.SL.2.1 Participate in collaborative conversations with diverse partners about *grade 2 topics and texts* with peers and adults in small and larger groups.									
CCSS.ELA-LITERACY.W.K.1 Use a combination of drawing, dictating, and writing to compose opinion pieces in which they tell a reader the topic or the name of the book they are writing about and state an opinion or preference about the topic or book (e.g., *My favorite book is ...*).									
CCSS.ELA-LITERACY.W.1.1 Write opinion pieces in which they introduce the topic or name the book they are writing about, state an opinion, supply a reason for the opinion, and provide some sense of closure.									
CCSS.ELA-LITERACY.W.2.1 Write opinion pieces in which they introduce the topic or book they are writing about, state an opinion, supply reasons that support the opinion, use linking words (e.g., *because, and, also*) to connect opinion and reasons, and provide a concluding statement or section.									
CCSS.ELA-LITERACY.W.K.2 Use a combination of drawing, dictating, and writing to compose informative/explanatory texts in which they name what they are writing about and supply some information about the topic.									
CCSS.ELA-LITERACY.W.1.2 Write informative/explanatory texts in which they name a topic, supply some facts about the topic, and provide some sense of closure.									
CCSS.ELA-LITERACY.W.2.2 Write informative/explanatory texts in which they introduce a topic, use facts and definitions to develop points, and provide a concluding statement or section.									

Common Core State Standards	Ch. 1	Ch. 2	Ch. 3	Ch. 4	Ch. 5	Ch. 6	Ch. 7	Ch. 8	Ch. 9
CCSS.ELA-LITERACY.W.K.7 Participate in shared research and writing projects (e.g., explore a number of books by a favorite author and express opinions about them).									
CCSS.ELA-LITERACY.W.1.7 Participate in shared research and writing projects (e.g., explore a number of "how-to" books on a given topic and use them to write a sequence of instructions).									
CCSS.ELA-LITERACY.W.2.7 Participate in shared research and writing projects (e.g., read a number of books on a single topic to produce a report; record science observations).									
CCSS.ELA-LITERACY.W.K.8 With guidance and support from adults, recall information from experiences or gather information from provided sources to answer a question.									
CCSS.ELA-LITERACY.W.1.8 With guidance and support from adults, recall information from experiences or gather information from provided sources to answer a question.									
CCSS.ELA-LITERACY.W.2.8 Recall information from experiences or gather information from provided sources to answer a question.									

Children's Books Cited

Capstone/Heinemann Library Books Cited

Anderson, S. (2015). *From seed to apple tree*. North Mankato, MN: Capstone.

Blair, E. (2012). My First Classic Story Series: *The boy who cried wolf: A retelling of Aesop's fable*. Minneapolis, MN: Capstone.

Braun, E. (2012). The Other Side of the Story Series: *Trust me, Jack's beanstalk stinks!: The story of Jack and the beanstalk as told by the giant*. Mankato, MN: Capstone.

deMarin, L. (2012). Wonder Readers Fluent Level Series: *Oranges: From fruit to juice*. Mankato, MN: Capstone.

Dickmann, N. (2010). Watch It Grow Series: *An apple's life*. Chicago, IL: Heinemann Library.

Dickmann, N. (2011). World of Farming Series: *Farm animals*. Chicago, IL: Heinemann Library.

Doyle, S. (2013). Farm Animals Series: *Cows*. North Mankato, MN: Capstone.

Dunn, M. (2012). South American Animals Series: *Llamas*. Mankato, MN: Capstone.

Englar, M. (2007). *Why do bears sleep all winter? A book about hibernation*. Mankato, MN: Capstone.

Freeman, M. (1999). Bears Series: *Brown bears*. Mankato, MN: Capstone.

Giulieri, A. (2015). Engage Literacy Assessment Series: *Kangaroos and their joeys*. Mankato, MN: Capstone.

Gunderson, J. (2014). The Other Side of the Story Series: *Really, Rapunzel needed a haircut!: The story of Rapunzel as told by Dame Gothel*. Minneapolis, MN: Capstone.

Hall, M. (2006). Patterns of Nature Series: *Hibernation*. Mankato, MN: Capstone.

Jones, C. (2011). My First Classic Story Series: *The little red hen: A retelling*. Mankato, MN: Capstone.

Kolpin, M. (2012). Bears Series: *American black bears*. Mankato, MN: Capstone.

Kolpin, M. (2012). Bears Series: *Grizzly bears*. Mankato, MN: Capstone.

Kolpin, M. (2012). Bears Series: *Polar Bears*. Mankato, MN: Capstone.

Kras, S. (2010). Australian Animal Series: *Koalas*. Mankato, MN: Capstone.

Kras, S. (2010). Australian Animal Series: *Wombats*. Mankato, MN: Capstone.

Lewis, C. (2015). Around the World Series: *Schools around the world*. Chicago, IL: Heinemann Library.

Loewen, N. (2012). The Other Side of the Story Series: *Believe me, Goldilocks rocks!: The story of the three bears as told by Baby Bear*. North Mankato, MN: Capstone.

Loewen, N. (2013). The Other Side of the Story Series: *No lie, I acted like a beast!: The story of Beauty and the Beast as told by the Beast*. North Mankato, MN: Capstone.

Loewen, N. (2014). The Other Side of the Story Series: *Frankly, I never wanted to kiss anybody: The story of the frog prince as told by the frog*. North Mankato, MN: Capstone.

Loewen, N. (2014). The Other Side of the Story Series: *No kidding, mermaids are a joke!: The story of the little mermaid as told by the prince*. North Mankato, MN: Capstone.

Manushkin, F. (2010). Katie Woo Series: *Boss of the world*. Minneapolis, MN: Capstone.

Mebane, J. (2013). Learn About Animal Behavior Series: *Animal hibernation*. North Mankato, MN: Capstone.

Nunn, D. (2011). From Trash to Treasures Series: *Cardboard*. Chicago, IL: Heinemann Library.

Nunn, D. (2011). From Trash to Treasures Series: *Paper*. Chicago, IL: Heinemann Library.

Nunn, D. (2011). From Trash to Treasures Series: *Plastic*. Chicago, IL: Heinemann Library.

Peterson, M. (2013). Animal Trackers Series: *Elephant seals*. Mankato, MN: Capstone.

Piumini, R. (2011). *The selfish giant*. Mankato, MN: Capstone.

Ready, D. (2014). Our Community Helpers Series: *Farmers help*. North Mankato, MN: Capstone.

Rissman, R. (2011). Animal Spikes and Spines Series: *Teeth*. Chicago, IL: Heinemann Library.

Rissman, R. (2014). Comparing Past and Present Series: *Going to school*. Chicago, IL: Heinemann Library.

Rissman, R. (2015). Night Safari Series: *Bats: Nocturnal flyers*. Chicago, IL: Heinemann Library.

Royston, A. (2013). Diary of a . . . Series: *Diary of a farmer*. Chicago, IL: Heinemann Library.

Rustad, M. (2016). Celebrate Winter Series: *All about animals in the winter*. North Mankato, MN: Capstone.

Schuh, M. (2011). How Fruit and Vegetables Grow Series: *Apples grow on a tree*. Mankato, MN: Capstone.

Schuh, M. (2011). Working Dogs Series: *Assistance dogs*. Mankato, MN: Capstone.

Shaskan, T. (2012). The Other Side of the Story Series: *Honestly, Red Riding Hood was rotten!: The story of Little Red Riding Hood as told by the wolf*. Mankato, MN: Capstone.

Shaskan, T. (2012). The Other Side of the Story Series: *Seriously, Cinderella is so annoying!: The story of Cinderella as told by the wicked stepmother*. Mankato, MN: Capstone.

Shores, E. (2011). Hands-On Science Fun Series: *How to make bubbles*. Mankato, MN: Capstone.

Shores, E. (2016). Celebrate Fall Series: *Apples*. Mankato, MN: Capstone.

Sirota, L. (2010). Australian Animals Series: *Bandicoots*. Mankato, MN: Capstone.

Smith, S. (2013). Take Care of Yourself Series: *Caring for your teeth*. Chicago, IL: Heinemann Library.

Thoennes Keller, K. (2005). From Farm to Table Series: *From apples to applesauce*. Mankato, MN: Capstone.

Thoennes Keller, K. (2005). From Farm to Table Series: *From peanuts to peanut butter*. Mankato, MN: Capstone.

White, M. (2012). My First Classic Story Series: *The ant and the grasshopper: A retelling of Aesop's fable*. Mankato, MN: Capstone.

Other Children's Books Cited

Artell, M. (2001). *Petite Rouge: A Cajun Red Riding Hood*. New York, NY: Dial Books for Young Readers.

Baer, E. (1990). *This is the way we go to school: A book about children around the world*. New York, NY: Scholastic.

Balestrino, P. (1989). *The skeleton inside you*. New York, NY: Crowell.

Bate, L. (1975). *Little Rabbit's loose tooth*. New York, NY: Crown.

Beeler, S. (1998). *Throw your tooth on the roof: Tooth traditions from around the world*. Boston, MA: Houghton Mifflin.

Beyer, E. (1995). "Jump and jiggle" (poem). https://movementandlearning.wordpress.com/2012/11/03 /jump-and-jiggle-by-evelyn-beyer-putting-poetry-in-motion/ (accessed January 11, 2016).

Blume, J. (1984). *The pain and the great one*. Scarsdale, NY: Bradbury Press.

Border, T. (2014). *Peanut Butter & Cupcake!* New York, NY: Philomel Books.

Bowdish, L. (2004). *George Washington Carver*. New York, NY: Children's Press.

Branley, F. (1987). *The moon seems to change*. New York, NY: Crowell.

Brown, M. (1971). *Cinderella*. New York, NY: Atheneum Books for Young Readers.

Brown, M. (1985). *Arthur's tooth*. New York, NY: Atlantic Monthly Press.

Cassino, M. & Nelson, J. (2009). *The story of snow: The science of winter's wonder*. San Francisco, CA: Chronicle Books.

Cech, J. (2007). *The princess and the pea*. New York, NY: Sterling.

Cook, L. (2011). *Peanut butter and homework sandwiches*. New York, NY: G.P. Putnam's Sons.

Cordell, M. (2009). *Trouble gum*. New York, NY: Feiwel and Friends.

Cox, L. (2014). *Elizabeth, queen of the seas*. New York, NY: Schwartz & Wade Books.

Crews, D. (1978). *Freight train*. New York, NY: Greenwillow Books.

Crews, D. (1982). *Harbor*. New York, NY: Greenwillow Books.

Cronin, D. (2000). *Click, clack, moo: Cows that type*. New York, NY: Simon & Schuster Books for Young Readers.

Cronin, D. (2002). *Giggle, giggle, quack*. New York, NY: Simon & Schuster Books for Young Readers.

Cronin, D. (2004). *Duck for president*. New York, NY: Simon & Schuster Books for Young Readers.

Cronin, D. (2006). *Dooby dooby moo*. New York, NY: Atheneum Books for Young Readers.

Crossingham, J. & Kalman, B. (2002). *What is hibernation?* New York, NY: Crabtree Publishers.

Daly, N. (2007). *Pretty Salma: A Little Red Riding Hood story from Africa*. New York, NY: Clarion Books.

Davies, N. (2001). *Bat loves the night*. Cambridge, MA: Candlewick Press.

Davies, N. (2001). *One tiny turtle*. Cambridge, MA: Candlewick Press.

De Capua, S. (2002). *We need directions!* New York, NY: Children's Press.

Delacroix, S. (2015). *Prickly Jenny*. Toronto, ON: Owlkids Books.

Demi (1990). *The empty pot*. New York, NY: H. Holt.

dePaola, T. (1992). *Jamie O'Rourke and the big potato: An Irish folktale*. New York, NY: Putnam.

Diakité, P. (2006). *I lost my tooth in Africa*. New York, NY: Scholastic Press.

Donaldson, J. (2003). *The spiffiest giant in town*. New York, NY: Dial Books for Young Readers.

Ehlert, L. (1987). *Growing vegetable soup*. New York, NY: HMH Books for Young Readers.

Ehlert, L. (1988). *Planting a rainbow*. San Diego, CA: Harcourt Brace Jovanovich.

Ehlert, L. (1995). *Snowballs*. San Diego, CA: Harcourt Brace.

Ehlert, L. (2001). *Waiting for wings*. San Diego, CA: Harcourt.

Emberley, E. (1972–2006). *Ed Emberley's Drawing Books (series)*. New York, NY: LB Kids.

Falk, L. (2010). *This is the way we go to school*. New York, NY: Children's Press.

Ferry, B. (2015). *Stick and Stone*. Boston, MA: Houghton Mifflin Harcourt.

Fowler, A. (1999). *A look at teeth*. New York, NY: Children's Press.

Fox, M. (1986). *Hattie and the fox*. New York, NY: Bradbury Press.

Fox, M. (1988). *Koala Lou*. San Diego, CA: Harcourt Brace Jovanovich.

Fox, M. (1993). *Possum magic*. New York, NY: HMH Books for Young Readers.

Fox, M. (1996). *Zoo-looking*. Greenvale, NY: Mondo Publishing.

Fox, M. (1997). *Whoever you are*. San Diego, CA: Harcourt Brace.

Fox, M. (2002). *The magic hat*. San Diego, CA: Harcourt.

Fox, M. (2004). *Where is the green sheep?* Orlando, FL: Harcourt.

Fox, M. (2005). *Hunwick's egg*. Orlando, FL: Harcourt.

Fox, M. (2009). *Hello, baby!* New York, NY: Beach Lane Books.

Galdone, P. (1972). *The three bears*. New York, NY: Seabury Press.

Grey, M. (2003). *The very smart pea and the princess-to-be*. New York, NY: Alfred A. Knopf.

Guarino, D. (1989). *Is your mama a llama?* New York, NY: Scholastic.

Hall, M. (2015). *Red: A crayon's story*. New York, NY: Greenwillow Books.

Henkes, K. (1987). *Sheila Rae, the brave*. New York, NY: Greenwillow Books.

Henkes, K. (2004). *Kitten's first full moon*. New York, NY: Greenwillow Books.

Hillert, M. (1982). *Little Red Riding Hood*. Chicago, IL: Follett Publishing.

Hills, T. (2006). *Duck & Goose*. New York, NY: Schwartz & Wade Books.

Hudson, C. & Sobol, R. (2006). *Construction zone*. Cambridge, MA: Candlewick Press.

Jenkins, S. & Page, R. (2006). *Move!* Boston, MA: Houghton Mifflin.

Judge, L. (2014). *Flight school*. New York, NY: Atheneum Books for Young Readers.

Kanarek, R. (2010). "I had a loose tooth" (poem). http://www.educationworld.com /a_earlychildhood/poems/poems043.shtml (accessed January 11, 2016).

Kasza, K. (1987). *The wolf's chicken stew*. New York, NY: Putnam.

Kasza, K. (2003). *My lucky day*. New York, NY: G.P. Putnam's Sons.

Keats, E. (1962). *The snowy day*. New York, NY: Viking Press.

Keats, E. (1964). *A whistle for Willie*. New York, NY: Viking Press.

Keats, E. (1967). *Peter's chair*. New York, NY: Harper & Row.

Keats, E. (1969). *Goggles!* New York, NY: Macmillan.

Keller, H. (2005). *Farfellina & Marcel*. New York, NY: Greenwillow Books.

Keller, L. (2000). *Open wide: Tooth school inside*. New York, NY: Henry Holt.

Kellogg, S. (1991). *Jack and the beanstalk*. New York, NY: Morrow Junior Books.

Kittinger, J. (2005). *George Washington Carver*. New York, NY: Children's Press.

Kosara, T. (2012). *Hibernation*. New York, NY: Scholastic.

Krauss, R. (1945). *The carrot seed*. New York, NY: Harper & Brothers.

LaBella, S. (2008). "Me and my skeleton" (poem). http://www.educationworld.com /a_earlychildhood/poems/poems043.shtml (accessed January 11, 2016).

Lionni, L. (1963). *Swimmy*. New York, NY: Pantheon.

Lionni, L. (1967). *Frederick*. New York, NY: Pantheon.

Lipson, E. (2009). *Applesauce season*. New York, NY: Roaring Brook Press.

Lichtenheld, T. (2012). *What mess?* New York, NY: Little, Brown Books for Young Readers.

Litwin, E. (2010). *Pete the cat: I love my white shoes*. New York, NY: Harper.

Lobel, A. (1970). *Frog and toad are friends*. New York, NY: Harper & Row.

Lovell, P. (2001). *Stand tall, Molly Lou Melon*. New York, NY: G.P. Putnam's Sons.

Lynch, W. (2003). *Whose teeth are these?* Milwaukee, WI: Gareth Stevens Publishing.

Lyon, G. (2011). *All the water in the world*. New York, NY: Atheneum Books for Young Readers.

Markle, S. (2013). *What if you had animal teeth!?* New York, NY: Scholastic.

Markle, S. (2014). *What if you had animal hair!?* New York, NY: Scholastic.

Markle, S. (2015). *What if you had animal feet!?* New York, NY: Scholastic.

Marsh, L. (2011). *Sea turtles*. Washington, DC: National Geographic.

McBeath, B. (2010). *The enormous turnip*. New York, NY: Scholastic.

McCarthy, M. (2010). *Pop!: The invention of bubble gum*. New York, NY: Simon & Schuster Books for Young Readers.

McDonnell, P. (2014). *A perfectly messed-up story*. New York, NY: Little, Brown and Company.

McKissack, P. (1986). *Flossie and the fox*. New York, NY: Dial Books for Young Readers.

McKissack, P. & McKissack, F. (1991). *George Washington Carver: The peanut scientist*. Hillside, NJ: Enslow Publishers.

McQueen, L. (1985). *The little red hen*. New York, NY: Scholastic.

Miller, A. (2009). *What does the president do?* New York, NY: Scholastic News.

Minor, W. & Minor, F. (2013). "If you were a panda bear" (poem), in *If you were a panda bear*. New York, NY: Katherine Tegen Books.

Montalván, L. & Witter, B. (2014). *Tuesday tucks me in: The loyal bond between a soldier and his service dog*. New York, NY: Roaring Brook Press.

Moore, H. (1997). "The water cycle" (poem). https://www.facebook.com/notes/summit-on-the -summit/the-water-cycle-poem-by-helen-h-moore-12-yrs-old/10150157678308685/ (accessed January 11, 2016).

Morris, A. (1989). *Bread, bread, bread*. New York, NY: Lothrop, Lee & Shepard Books.

Morris, A. (1990). *On the go*. New York, NY: Lothrop, Lee & Shepard Books.

Nelson, R. (2011). *Hibernation*. Minneapolis, MN: Lerner.

Nodset, J. (1963). *Who took the farmer's hat?* New York, NY: Harper & Row.

Nolan, J. (2014). *PB & J hooray!: Your sandwich's amazing journey from farm to table*. Chicago, IL: Albert Whitman & Company.

O'Connor, J. (2006). *Fancy Nancy*. New York, NY: HarperCollins.

Parkes, B. & Smith, J. (1986). *The enormous watermelon*. Melbourne, Australia: Crystal Lake.

Pett, M. (2014). *The girl and the bicycle*. New York, NY: Simon & Schuster Books for Young Readers.

Pinkney, J. (2007). *Little Red Riding Hood*. New York, NY: Little, Brown.

Posada, M. (2007). *Guess what is growing inside this egg?* Minneapolis, MN: Millbrook Press.

Rathmann, P. (1995). *Officer Buckle and Gloria*. New York, NY: Putnam's.

Rocco, J. (2014). *Blizzard*. Los Angeles, CA: Disney-Hyperion.

Rosenthal, A. (2013). *Exclamation mark*. New York, NY: Scholastic Press.

Roza, G. (2006). *The peanut butter party*. New York, NY: Rosen Publishing Group.

Ryder, J. (2009). *Panda kindergarten*. New York, NY: Collins.

Salem, L. & Stewart, J. (2004). *Kookaburra*. Elizabethtown, PA: Continental Press.

Schertle, A. (2002). *All you need for a snowman*. San Diego, CA: Harcourt.

Schmidt, K. (1986). *Little Red Riding Hood*. New York, NY: Scholastic.

Scieszka, J. (1989). *The true story of the 3 little pigs by A. Wolf*. New York, NY: Viking Kestrel.

Sendak, M. (1963). *Where the wild things are*. New York, NY: Harper & Row.

Seuss, D. (1981). *The tooth book*. New York, NY: Random House.

Shannon, D. (1998). *No, David!* New York, NY: Blue Sky Press.

Silverman, E. (1992). *Big pumpkin*. New York, NY: Macmillan.

Slobodkina, E. (1985). *Caps for sale: A tale of a peddler, some monkeys, and their monkey business*. New York, NY: Harper & Row.

Snyder, I. (2003). *Wax to crayons*. New York, NY: Children's Press.

Stevens, J. & Stevens Crummel, S. (2005). *Cook-a-doodle-doo!* Boston, MA: HMH Books for Young Readers.

St. George, J. (2000). *So you want to be president?* New York, NY: Philomel Books.

Sturges, P. (1999). *The little red hen makes a pizza*. New York, NY: Dutton Children's Books.

Sweeney, J. (1996). *Me on the map*. New York, NY: Crown.

Taus-Bolstad, S. (2013). *From milk to ice cream*. Minneapolis, MN: Lerner Publications Company.

Taus-Bolstad, S. (2013). *From wheat to bread*. Minneapolis, MN: Lerner Publications Company.

Urban, L. (2015). *Little Red Henry*. Somerville, MA: Candlewick Press.

Vestergaard, H. (2013). "The cherry picker" (poem), in *Digger, dozer, dumper*. Cambridge, MA: Candlewick Press.

Waddell, M. (1992). *Farmer duck*. Cambridge, MA: Candlewick Press.

Waddell, M. (1996). *The pig in the pond*. Cambridge, MA: Candlewick Press.

Walters, V. (1999). *Are we there yet, Daddy?* New York, NY: Viking.

Ward, J. (2014). *Mama built a little nest*. New York, NY: Beach Lane Books.

Watt, M. (2008). *Scaredy squirrel*. Toronto, ON: Kids Can Press.

Westcott, N. (1987). *Peanut butter and jelly: A play rhyme*. New York, NY: E. P. Dutton.

Willems, M. (2010). *City dog, country frog*. New York, NY: Hyperion Books for Children.

Willems, M. (2007–). Elephant and Piggie Series (various).

Wilson, K. (2002). *Bear snores on*. New York, NY: Margaret K. McElderry Books.

Wilson, K. (2003). *Bear wants more*. New York, NY: Matgaret K. McElderry Books.

Wilson, K. (2006). *Bear's new friend*. New York, NY: Margaret K. McElderry Books.

Wilson, K. (2007). *Bear feels sick*. New York, NY: Margaret K. McElderry Books.

Wilson, K. (2008). *Bear feels scared*. New York, NY: Margaret K. McElderry Books.

Wilson, K. (2008). *Bear stays up for Christmas*. New York, NY: Margaret K. McElderry Books.

Wilson, K. (2011). *Bear's loose tooth*. New York, NY: Margaret K. McElderry Books.

Wilson, K. (2012). *Bear says thanks*. New York, NY: Margaret K. McElderry Books.

Woodson, J. (2012). *Each kindness*. New York, NY: Nancy Paulsen Books.

Woodson, J. (2014). *Brown girl dreaming*. New York, NY: Nancy Paulsen Books.

Yolen, J. (2000). *How do dinosaurs say good night?* New York, NY: Blue Sky Press.

Yolen, J. (2011). *Creepy monsters, sleepy monsters: A lullaby*. Somerville, MA: Candlewick Press.

Yolen, J. (2013). *Romping monsters, stomping monsters*. Sommerville, MA: Candlewick Press.

Young, E. (1989). *Lon Po Po: A Red-Riding Hood story from China*. New York, NY: Philomel Books.

Ziefert, H. (2000). *Little Red Riding Hood*. New York, NY: Viking.

References

Barr, C. & Harbison, C. (2011). "Book title output and average prices: 2007–2010," in *The library and trade book almanac*. Medford, NJ: Information Today Inc.

Britton, J. (1970). *Language and learning*. Coral Gables, FL: University of Miami Press.

Camp, D. (2000). It takes two: Teaching twin texts of fact and fiction. *The Reading Teacher*, 53, 400–408.

Costley, K. & West, H. (2012). Teaching practice: A perspective on inter-text and prior knowledge. *Southeastern Regional Association of Teacher Educators Journal*, 21, 21–24.

Fox, M. (1992). *Dear Mem Fox, I have read all your books even the pathetic ones: And other incidents in the life of a children's book author*. San Diego, CA: Harcourt Brace Jovanovich.

Gutkind, L. (1997). *The art of creative nonfiction: Writing and selling the literature of reality*. New York, NY: Wiley.

National Governors Association Center for Best Practices & Council of Chief State School Officers (2010). Common Core State Standards for English language arts and literacy in history/social studies, science, and technical subjects. Washington, DC: Authors.

Orwell, G. (1946). *Animal farm*. New York, NY: Harcourt, Brace and Company.

Pearson, P. & Gallagher, M. (1983). The instruction of reading comprehension. *Contemporary Educational Psychology*, 8 (3), 317–344.

Short, K., Hartse, J., & Burke, C. (1996) *Creating classrooms for authors and inquirers*. Portsmouth, NH: Heinemann.

Soalt, J. (2005). Bringing together fictional and informational texts to improve comprehension. *Reading Teacher*, 58 (7), 680–683.

Sweller, J., Van Merriënboer, J., & Paas, F. (1998). Cognitive architecture and instructional design. *Educational Psychology Review*, 10 (3), 251–296.

Tyler, A. (2015). *A spool of blue thread*. New York, NY: Knopf.

Wilkerson, I. (2010). *The warmth of other suns: The epic story of America's great migration*. New York, NY: Random House.

Willis, J. (2015, February 2). Play brain games to help your child learn to read. *Parent ToolKit* (blog). http://www.parenttoolkit.com/index.cfm?objectid=326573E0-A7E0-11E4-B6B70050569A5318 (accessed November 22, 2015).

Wolf, A. (2012, August 21). *Once there was a poem that knew the facts*. http://www.allanwolf.com/visits/poetry-and-nonfiction (accessed December 12, 2015).

Notes

Notes

Maupin House
capstone

At Maupin House by Capstone Professional, we continue to look for professional development resources that support grades K–8 classroom teachers in areas, such as these:

Literacy	Language Arts
Content-Area Literacy	Research-Based Practices
Assessment	Inquiry
Technology	Differentiation
Standards-Based Instruction	School Safety
Classroom Management	School Community

If you have an idea for a professional development resource, visit our Become an Author website at:

http://www.capstonepub.com/classroom/professional-development/become-an-author/

There are two ways to submit questions and proposals.

1. You may send them electronically to: proposals@capstonepd.com

2. You may send them via postal mail. Please be sure to include a self-addressed stamped envelope for us to return materials.

Acquisitions Editor
Capstone Professional
1 N. LaSalle Street, Suite 1800
Chicago, IL 60602